# NO DEAL temptations

REAL DEAL bible studies


## AUTHORS

Len Aurich

Kurt Bickel

Tom Couser

Rich Gutekunst

Mike Heinz

Kirk Hille

Sally Hiller

William Moorehead

Kevin Popp

Jay Reed

Ron Roma

Cindy Wheeler

## EDITOR

Mark Sengele


CONCORDIA PUBLISHING HOUSE • SAINT LOUIS

*Your comments and suggestions concerning the material are appreciated. Please write the Editor of Youth Materials, Concordia Publishing House, 3558 S. Jefferson Avenue, St. Louis, MO 63118-3968.*

*This publication may also be available in braille, in large print, or on cassette tape for the visually impaired. Please allow 8 to 12 weeks for delivery. Write to Library for the Blind, 1333 S. Kirkwood Road, St. Louis, MO 63122-7295; call 1-800-433-3954, ext. 1322; or e-mail to blind.library@lcms.org.*



*Manufactured in the United States of America.*



*1 2 3 4 5 6 7 8 9 10 12 11 10 09 08 07 06 05 04 03*

# Table of Contents

# INTRODUCTION

## WELCOME TO THE REAL DEAL SERIES!

Welcome to the Real Deal! Each of the books in this series presents 12 lessons that focus on the Gospel and the Word of God, the Real Deal. Each book in the series has a theme around which the lessons are organized. (For an outline of the Real Deal Series, look inside the back cover of this book.)

* ***The topics*** *are* real. *Each lesson deals with* real *issues in the lives of young people and is grounded in God's Word.*

* ***The leader's materials*** *are easy to use. Each lesson is completely outlined and designed for* real *success in teaching. Leader's directions are clear and easy to follow. Materials needed for teaching are easily obtained. Many lessons contain additional materials for times when students finish quickly.*

* ***Student pages*** *are reproducible so teachers can copy the number they really need.*

* *And, finally, the* **power of the Gospel** *is at the core of every study. Students will see God's Word as the* real *source of information for their everyday lives.*

## ABOUT THIS BOOK

### No Deal

Each of the 12 studies in this book deals with temptations that many young people face. Many of these issues can be very sensitive for young people to deal with. Use care in your approach to each study so that God's truths remain objective and your care for each student becomes personalized.

The studies are designed for use with students in the ninth through twelfth grades. More mature junior high students may also benefit from these studies. Each study is a complete unit. Lessons may be used in any order. While designed for the typical one-hour Bible class, these studies may be adapted for other youth ministry settings. For example, selected studies could form the core of material for a youth night or retreat.

## PREPARING TO TEACH

Each lesson has a *Lesson Focus* and a *Gospel Focus* statement at the beginning. These help the leader understand the lesson topic and direction.

The *Lesson Outline* provides a quick look at the study and a list of materials needed for each segment of the lesson.

The *Lesson Activities* include large- and small-group discussion, opportunities for individual study, and active-learning suggestions.

Most lessons also contain background information to assist the leader in preparing for the class time. Class leaders should review the entire lesson in advance of the class time.

It is assumed that the Bible class leader will have the usual basic classroom equipment and supplies available—pencils or pens for each student, blank paper (and occasionally tape or marking pens), and a chalkboard or its equivalent (white board, overhead transparency projector, or newsprint pad and easel) with corresponding markers or chalk. Encourage the students to bring their own Bibles. Then they can mark useful passages and make notes to guide their personal Bible study and reference. Do provide additional Bibles, however, for visitors or students who do not bring one. The appropriate Student Page should be copied in a quantity sufficient for the class and distributed at the time indicated in the leader's notes.

The studies are outlined completely in the leader's notes, including a suggested length of time recommended for each section of the study. The suggested times will total 50–60 minutes, the maximum amount most Sunday-morning Bible classes have available. Each session begins with an opening activity that may or may not be indicated on the Student Page. Teachers who regularly begin with prayer should include it before the opening activity. Most other parts of the study, except the closing prayer, are indicated in both the Leader Guide and on the Student Page.

An average class size of 10 students is assumed. To facilitate discussion, especially when your class is larger than average, it is recommended to conduct much of the discussion in smaller groups—pairs, triads, or groups of no more than five or six. Instructions to that effect are often included in the guide. If your class is small, you are already a small group and can ignore any such suggestions.

Some lessons contain bonus suggestions. Use these when the study progresses more quickly than expected, when your normal session exceeds 50–60 minutes, or when a suggested activity doesn't work with your group. They can also be used during the week.

Of course, the leader is encouraged to review the study thoroughly, well in advance of its presentation. Then the materials can be tailored to your individual students' needs and preferences as well as your own preferred teaching style.

## TIPS FOR LEADERS OF YOUTH BIBLE STUDIES

One challenge of leading a youth Bible study is the need for relevant, Christ-centered, effective study material. An equal challenge is growing in one's ability to teach and lead effectively. While the studies in the Real Deal Series are intended to meet the first challenge, the material in this section is intended to help you meet the second challenge.

Skim this section for ideas that spark your interest. Or read it completely. Either way, you'll find support to help young people grow in God's Word.

### The Power of Forgiveness

Our human nature is fascinated with power. We marvel at it in nature, strive for it for ourselves, and fear it in others. Power struggles are at the root of much of humanity's distress. And who hasn't longed at one time or another for the power to change things—to right a wrong, improve a circumstance, or correct a fault?

As leaders of youth Bible study, we share in that universal desire. We seek through the time we spend with young people in the study of God's Word to *change their lives*—to impart or increase the assurance of salvation, to improve knowledge of Scripture, to change sinful behavior.

Since we seek that kind of change, it is helpful to ask and answer a simple question—"What has the power to change lives?"

**Our Lives Need to Change**

It is certainly true that change is needed in the lives of all human creatures. Because of our sinful nature, we are not the perfect people God created us to be. The apostle Paul recognized this truth in his own life when he lamented, "What I want to do I do not do, but what I hate I do" (Romans 7:15).

Young people recognize this truth in their lives. They are confronted daily with temptations of all kinds, and like all of us, they succumb to it more often than they'd like. They experience the result of sin in the lives of others as well—rejection by friends, divorce between parents, and violence in all parts of their lives.

**The Blessing of Forgiveness!**

"Who will rescue me from this body of death?" Paul asks (Romans 7:24). "Thanks be to God—through Jesus Christ our Lord!" (verse 25). Through Jesus Christ we have the only power that can change sinful lives—the forgiveness of sins and newness of life.

Human effort cannot change lives (Galatians 2:20). Adherence to laws and regulations cannot (Romans 3:23). Only the power of Christ at work in our hearts through the Gospel, the assurance of forgiveness through the suffering and death of Jesus Christ, can bring about change in lives twisted by sin. Young people and adults encounter that Gospel message of forgiveness through studying God's Word, sharing in confession and forgiveness in Christian worship, and receiving God's blessings in Baptism and Holy Communion. And their lives are changed! God lifts the weight of sin and gives them the power to live faithful lives.

**Eternal Significance**

Our time with the young people in our Bible classes is limited. We have 60 minutes or less, once or twice a week . . . or month . . . or year. Certainly no time to spare. Therefore, in each lesson we want to proclaim a clear message of forgiveness in Christ for all who believe in Christ and repent of their sins through the power of the Holy Spirit. Specific application of this Gospel message is critical every time we teach.

As you prepare to teach each week, look for that message of forgiveness in the Scripture passages and the Bible study you will teach. Share the Gospel clearly. And pray that God will help you plant seeds for change in the lives of the young people you teach.

**Keys to Classroom Discipline**

Discipline—by which most teachers probably mean having control of a teaching situation, having a minimum of disruptions, and keeping the interest of their students—is a nearly universal concern among volunteer teachers.

Here are some things teachers should *Prepare, Know, Use,* and *Avoid*. They are the real keys to classroom discipline.

**Prepare**

It will come as no surprise to most teachers that an ounce of preparation prevents a pound of cure.

* Prepare yourself. *Think through past study sessions. Identify discipline situations and analyze them. Then you can choose from among the other hints that follow.*

* Prepare the space. *Be alert for frequent distractions (a stack of magazines, a busy window, an uncomfortable chair) and work to eliminate them. Watch for other physical arrangements that distract. Are some chairs out of your line of sight? Rearrange them. Do certain students always sit together and distract each other? Talk with them privately and offer to separate them. Do you usually sit near the door, while students look over your shoulder at the traffic? Try sitting opposite the door to draw students' attention away from the distraction. Do you frequently rely on writing activities? Have tables or clipboards in your classroom to facilitate things. Your attention to these details will contribute to a disciplined classroom.*

* Prepare the lesson. *When the teacher is well prepared, has materials ready to go, and moves promptly from one section of the lesson to another, he or she avoids "down time" that could tempt students to misbehave or cause frustration. Attention is maintained, and most discipline situations never have a chance to get off the ground.*

* Prepare the lesson with your group in mind. *Provide time for the students to meet their social need to talk among themselves before or after class. Incorporate active learning experiences and use small-group discussion as frequently as possible to keep all students involved. Keep material relevant to the lives of the students.*

**Know**

* *It is important to* know the policies *for dealing with disruptions in your church and educational setting. If no policies seem to be in effect, suggest to your superintendent or board of Christian education that such policies would be helpful. When should a disruptive student be removed from class? How should this be done? Is a system of cautions to the student suggested or required?*

* Know your students. *Knowing their names, interests, learning difficulties, and preferences will greatly assist you as you teach. Consider a personal visit or phone call. Be sensitive to those things that could embarrass a student or make him or her uncomfortable in class.*

* Know the parents. *Make a point to talk to them at church, by phone, or in a home visit. The information you gain will be invaluable. Also, should a discipline situation arise, it won't be your first contact with them.*

**Use**

Use techniques to head off difficult situations in the class.

* Divert *a student from misbehavior by giving responsibility, asking for an opinion, or adapting an activity to interest the student directly. One teacher of teens covers the study table with newsprint each week and distributes markers. Students are allowed to doodle to their heart's content, as long as class is not disrupted and they pay attention and participate.*

* Affirm *students as frequently as possible. Catch them being good, and then compliment them. Make sure that even the disruptive student knows that it is the behavior—not him or her—that you find undesirable or unacceptable.*

* *Use* peers *as partners in discipline. Allow your students to participate in setting guidelines for classroom behavior. Invite them to help each other participate fully in class and to discourage unwanted behavior. Ask, "How can we get the most out of these study sessions?" (Listen carefully to their responses.)*

* *Gain* assistance from others. *Ask experienced teachers, parents, and administrators for help in solving discipline problems. Don't think you are the only one who has problems. There is no stigma in asking for help to be a better teacher.*

**Avoid**

While we're at it, there are several things you'll want to avoid.

* Avoid threats. *Threats of punishment are unlikely to impact teens. "If you don't cooperate, I'll . . ." is usually a hollow threat. Instead, if the action is necessary, take it without threatening. Failure to follow through on even one threat makes all others less credible.*

* Avoid put-downs. *When in the middle of conflict, it is tempting to resort to attacks. "You're the worst class I've ever had" does little to bring out the best in students of any age. (They may soon live up to your evaluation.) Instead, compliment good behavior, ignore misbehavior if it is not truly disruptive, and deal with difficult students respectfully.*

* Avoid physical contact. *It seems unlikely in a volunteer teaching situation that such contact would occur or be beneficial. Long before this possibility develops, seek assistance from others in determining guidelines.*

* Avoid overreaction. *Young people frequently find and push our "hot buttons"—the behaviors or issues that evoke an emotional reaction that gets in the way of good judgment. Try to stay objective about discipline. Be willing to ask yourself or another teacher, Is this really a big deal?*

**Final Thoughts**

* Be flexible! *Many a potential discipline problem can be headed off by a change of activity or direction in the middle of a lesson. When you sense things getting out of hand, "flex" your lesson plan.*

* Be loving. *Let the forgiveness we have in Christ be evident in your behavior as well as in your lessons. Even discipline situations can be opportunities to share the Gospel of Jesus Christ.*

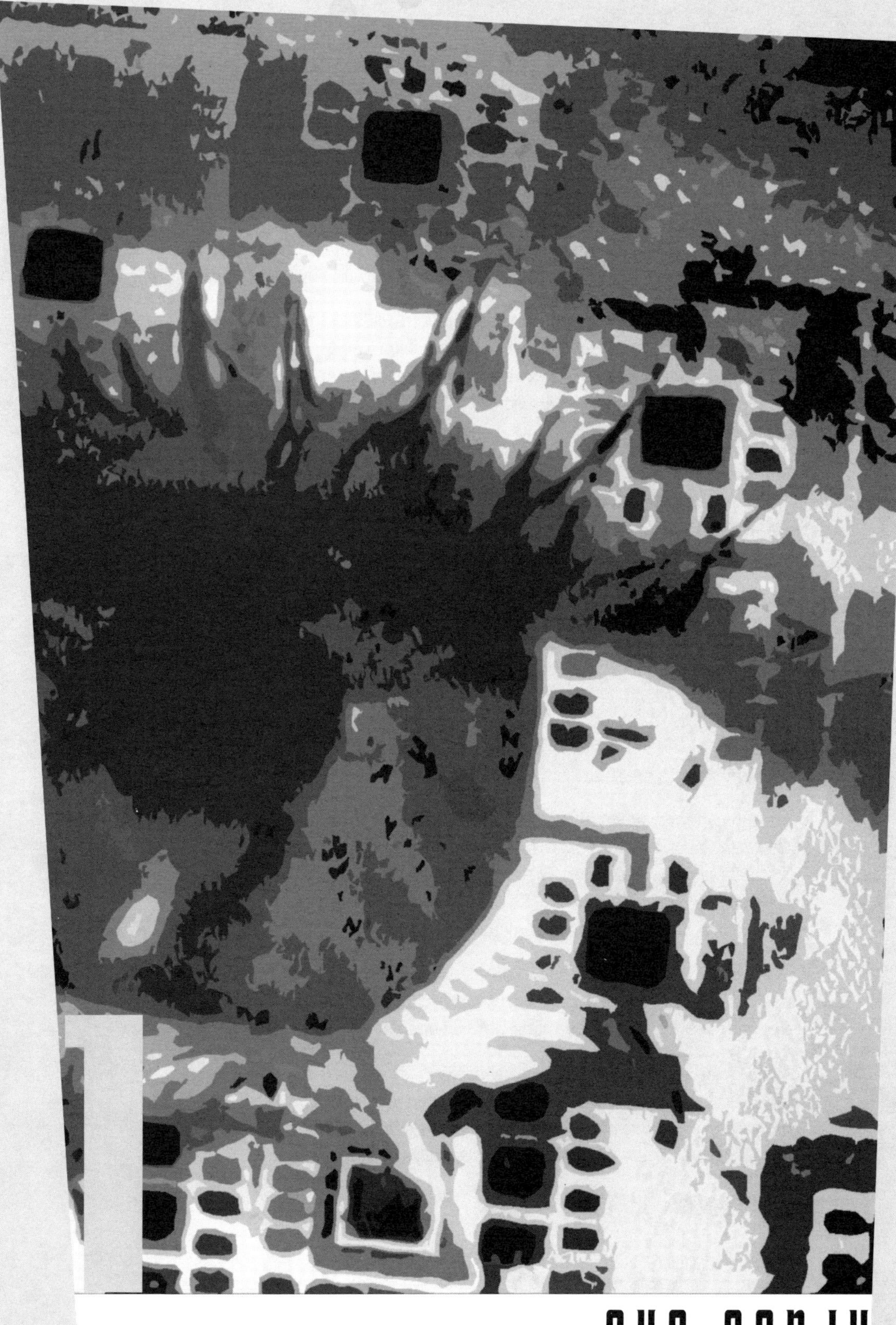

# 1

# eye candy

pornography

## LESSON FOCUS

Lust lies at the heart of many sins. As young people deal with their developing sexuality, they confront the troublesome issue of pornography, which involves lust. Sexual lust reduces the subject of our desire to an image, which we use and abuse, rather than as a person for whom we care and to whom we can relate in wholesome ways. The difference between sinful lust and healthy desire is one of attitude and the action we take in response to our desire.

## GOSPEL FOCUS

Christian attitudes and actions flow from the presence and power of Christ at work in us as we study His Word and receive strength through His means of grace. As we repent of sinful desires and receive Jesus' forgiveness, the Holy Spirit strengthens our faith, enabling us to choose "noble" alternatives in our lives.

## Lesson Outline

| ACTIVITY | SUGGESTED TIME | MATERIALS NEEDED |
|---|---|---|
| *Eye Candy* | *10 minutes* | *Newsprint or board* |
| *What Scripture Says* | *15 minutes* | *Copies of Student Page, Bibles* |
| *Where Does Lust Lead?* | *15 minutes* | *Copies of Student Page, newsprint* |
| *What If It Were You?* | *15 minutes* | *Copies of Student Page* |
| *Confessing* | *5 minutes* | *None* |

## A NOTE TO THE LEADER

Pray for God's blessing on your preparation and conduct of this particular session. Be familiar with what is taught in the passages that form the biblical basis for this session, as well as the other passages in the leader materials. Young people may be hesitant to discuss this area of temptation. Consider how much you are willing to share with your class about the struggles you have in this area of your life and how your Christian faith helps you deal with them. Make advance arrangements for your pastor's participation in the closing section of this lesson.

## EYE CANDY (10 MINUTES)

On the board or newsprint have students list the things in their life that tempt them sexually and cause them to stray from God's design and desire for our use of His gift of sexuality. Encourage students to be honest and forthright. They may immediately mention reading material with sexual content. Videos, movies, television, the Internet, advertising of all kinds, the systems and institutions of our culture, the behavior of others (how they dress, what they encourage us to do, etc.), the devil, and the sinful self (our own sinful desires of heart and mind to which we give in and commit sin) can tempt us to sin sexually. Ask, "How readily accessible are these sources of temptation? Why do you think these items are such a powerful source of temptation?"

Offer a prayer that God will bless your study and give each participant the wisdom to discern His will and to apply faith and Christian conviction to the issue of sinful sexual desire.

## WHAT SCRIPTURE SAYS (15 MINUTES)

Distribute copies of the Student Page. Form small groups, and assign each group one or more of the passages. Ask them to find and read the passage(s) and summarize what it says regarding sinful sexual desire—lust. Have students keep in mind these two general questions: What is God saying? How should we as Christians respond?

Two basic Scripture passages on the topic of lust (sinful sexual desire) are Matthew 5:27–28 and Colossians 3:5. The New Testament alone has plenty more to say on the topic, given that there are approximately 50 passages that speak of lust, adultery, immorality, and fornication. St. Paul includes major sections in his Letters on relations between the sexes, especially in 1 Corinthians 6 and 7. If one looks at the commandments, not only does lust have an obvious connection to the Sixth Commandment, but it is also an issue for at least the First, Ninth, and Tenth as well. Jesus in Matthew 5:27–28 broadens the boundaries of the Sixth Commandment to include the intentions of the heart, the motives of the inner, sinful self. Jesus wants to fence off immoral behavior not only where it ends, but also where it starts (see also Mark 7:1–23 for Jesus' opinion of where immoral behavior begins). In Colossians 3:5 Paul speaks to Christians who live in the power of the Spirit and who, therefore, can heed the admonition to turn their backs on what violates who they are in the sight of God.

Help your students see that by faith they live in the Spirit (by God's grace) and therefore know God's love and power, which motivates them to confess sin, to receive God's forgiveness, and to shun the sin that always lies in wait (Genesis 4:7).

Emphasize that through faith in Christ Jesus, God offers full and complete forgiveness for all sins, including sexual sins. Forgiveness is theirs, as Romans 8:1–4 clearly states. Remember, the Word of God is our means of evaluating the intentions of our hearts (Hebrews 4:12).

## WHERE DOES LUST LEAD? (15 MINUTES)

Ask, "What negative behaviors result from the failure of people to remain sexually pure? Where does lust lead us?"

Give the students a few minutes to work in small groups or individually to write responses on the Student Page. Then invite volunteers to share their responses. List the responses on the board or newsprint. They may include production and use of pornography, rape, voyeurism, confusion and lowering of community moral standards, masturbation, divorce, sexual addiction, child sexual abuse, stalking, prostitution, experimenting with homosexual acts, adultery, and premarital sex.

Note those that are selected as most troublesome. Listen to the suggestions for dealing with these problems in your community. Look for a practical corrective measure that your class might be capable of achieving as an activity outside of class.

Deal sensitively with these issues. Be aware that some of your students may have been victims of sexual abuse or may be sexually active. Don't put people on the spot, but do encourage them to share their opinions honestly.

## WHAT IF IT WERE YOU? (15 MINUTES)

Read the situation described on the Student Page. Invite two volunteers to act out the situation, doing their best to reflect the attitudes and concerns as described. Then invite other members of the class to comment on how realistically each role was played. Which statements seemed on target? Where might the dialogue have changed? Especially affirm the forgiveness that God offers to all who repent of sin and the power for resisting temptations, which results from Christ at work in us through God's Word.

If your students are unlikely to succeed in a role play, discuss the situation in small groups. Ask students to prepare actual statements the parent and youth might make. After a few minutes, ask each group to report, and discuss their responses as described above.

## CONFESSING (5 MINUTES)

Ask your pastor to come to class and conclude it with a brief service of confession and forgiveness (*Lutheran Worship,* pages 308–9). Make sure your pastor knows what you have been discussing and what sins will be on your students' minds. This should not be a public confession of previously private and unknown sins. Your pastor will know how to give people time to confess before God, even in silence. Ask him to share with the class why we confess our sin and receive forgiveness in a public worship service. He may wish to offer private time for any student who needs it.

## IF YOU HAVE MORE TIME

Invite to your class an attorney or juvenile-court judge who is knowledgeable about how many adolescents run into legal trouble in your community or county because of inappropriate sexual behavior. Have students prepare questions ahead of time. Such questions as "How much pornographic material is in the hands of senior high youth?" or "How many adolescents have been convicted in our community of sexual crimes in the past year?" are appropriate.

# I. Eye Candy

## What Scripture Says

*Genesis 4:7*

*Matthew 5:27–28*

*Romans 8:1–4*

*1 Corinthians 7:1–40*

*Hebrews 4:12*

*Exodus 20:1–17*

*Mark 7:1–23*

*1 Corinthians 6:9–20*

*Colossians 3:5*

*What is God saying?* *How should we as Christians respond?*

## Where Does Lust Lead?

*List all the kinds of behaviors to which lust, or sinful sexual desire, may lead. Then pick the one you think is the biggest problem for high school students today. Be prepared to explain why you think so.*

*What could cause positive changes in the moral behavior of your community's high school youth?*

*How can your ideas be effectively implemented? Is there something specific your church or youth group can do?*

## What If It Were You?

*A parent and his/her 15-year-old high school student are in the middle of a discussion. While checking the computer's history file, the parent discovered a Web site with sexually explicit pictures and content. The parent confronts the teen and asks why it is there. Imagine the conversation that follows.*

*What would each person say? What are the issues involved? What are each person's feelings?*

*What points must the parent make? How will the student defend himself/herself? What admissions should he/she make?*

*Assume that this family is Christian. How might sin, forgiveness, and faith be part of this discussion? How would the discussion end?*

# 2

# too little of a good thing

## LESSON FOCUS

All people have boundaries or limits to areas of touch, closeness, and intimacy within which they feel comfortable. Young people benefit from knowing their personal boundaries, making choices about what is appropriate in the context of their Christian faith, and knowing what they will do when they or others cross those boundaries.

## GOSPEL FOCUS

God in His mercy, through Jesus, forgives us our sexual sins, just as He forgives all other sin. The Holy Spirit empowers us to establish and keep the sexual boundaries God established for us in His Word. We need to make constructive choices also in this area.

## Lesson Outline

| ACTIVITY | SUGGESTED TIME | MATERIALS NEEDED |
|---|---|---|
| *Full Disclosure* | *10 minutes* | *Cans or boxes of food* |
| *Sex and the Media/ Sex and Teen Culture* | *10 minutes* | *Copies of Student Page* |
| *Youth Temptations* | *10 minutes* | *Copies of Student Page, Bibles* |
| *Sex and God's Word* | *15 minutes* | *Copies of Student Page, Bibles* |
| *Optional—Digging Deeper* | *15 minutes* | *Copies of Bonus Student Page, Bibles* |
| *Closing* | *5 minutes* | *Bible* |

## A NOTE FOR THE LEADER

Statistics suggest that some of the students in any group of young people will already be sexually active. Don't assume all the youth in your class are exceptions to this rule. Deal with the matter of chastity frankly, but show love and concern for any who have already committed sexual sin. Show them that God is always ready to forgive those who repent of sin. Make yourself or another resource available for private discussion and counsel.

## FULL DISCLOSURE (10 MINUTES)

Bring enough food cans or boxes so that each student or pair of students will have one to look at. Give each student, or pair of students, a can or box of food. Have them examine the label and note the kinds of information printed on the can (ingredients, nutritional content, brand name, etc.). List the label information on newsprint or a chalkboard. Ask, "Why do manufacturers list all this information on the label?" (Required by law; to protect the consumer.)

Ask, "What if we had to have such full disclosure statements before becoming sexually active with someone? What kind of information would someone need to determine how 'at risk' he or she is before engaging in sexual behavior? What are some negative consequences of teens engaging in sexual behavior?" List these on a chalkboard or newsprint.

Tell the students that in today's session they will consider boundaries for teenage sexual behavior. Pray together for God to guide and direct the discussion according to His will, that students would be strengthened to do what God desires.

## SEX AND THE MEDIA/SEX AND TEEN CULTURE (10 MINUTES)

Have the students create groups of four to seven people. Assign each group either "Sex and the Media" or "Sex and Teen Culture" on the Student Page. After they break into their groups, ask each group to select a "reporter" to present the results of their discussion to the rest of the class. Give the reporter newsprint and a marker to record the results.

"Sex and the Media" calls for students to compile a list of sexual messages and attitudes promoted by the media. You may wish to have newspapers (the entertainment section) and magazines available.

"Sex and Teen Culture" suggests that students brainstorm a list of attitudes and suggest what percentage of students at their school might hold those attitudes (i.e., All virgins are prudes—30%).

After the groups have had about seven minutes to create their lists, ask each to report. Talk with the whole group about the lists they created. Ask, "What other items could you add? Are these realistic? How do you feel about that?" When assigning percentages to the second list of attitudes, encourage a quick and smooth decision. The intent is simply to raise issues, reach an approximate consensus, and move on, not to debate the scope of each attitude.

## YOUTH TEMPTATIONS (10 MINUTES)

With the whole group brainstorm the different ways teens are tempted sexually (rent/watch sexually explicit movies; look at pornographic books/magazines; tell "dirty stories"; swap stories of personal sexual exploits; go further than they should on a date). List the ways on the board or a piece of newsprint.

Brainstorm ways teens could avoid each temptation (avoid looking at video jackets of improper movies; read the Bible daily; when tempted, pray that Christ would remove temptation; don't go out with people who are known to be sexually active; ask friends to pray for them that they might resist temptation). List these ways on the board or other side of the newsprint.

## SEX AND GOD'S WORD (15 MINUTES)

Assign each small group one or more of the passages on the Student Page to read and discuss. After they have worked for about five minutes, ask each group to share their thoughts. The following comments should be added if not shared by others:

*1. The sex act virtually "marries" two people in God's eyes. Therefore sex between unmarried persons is immoral—sin. God does not leave us powerless. Because Jesus died for us on the cross in payment for our sin, the Holy Spirit now lives in us, offering strength against temptation.*

*2. David makes clear that his sin is against God. He asks for forgiveness and the opportunity for a new start. That's good news for youth who have become sexually active. God through His Word and Sacraments enables a heart to know His will, admit sin and failure, and in grace return to Him. God wants this for each of us.*

*3. God promises complete forgiveness, not anger, to repentant sinners.*

Summarize with words such as these: "The Bible is clear that sex outside of marriage is sin. Expression of physical affection between unmarried people is progressive. The further things go, the harder it is to stop. It is helpful to set boundaries with persons with whom we go out. God offers forgiveness for sin; He also offers strength to resist sin. How far is too far? Where will you draw the line? Create a boundary based on God's Word and pray for God's help to keep it."

## OPTIONAL—DIGGING DEEPER (15 MINUTES)

Distribute copies of the Bonus Student Page. Read, or have a volunteer reread,

1 Corinthians 6:12–20. Direct the small groups to share their responses to the questions that follow on the Bonus Student Page. After a few minutes invite small groups to share responses to each of the questions. Include the following comments in the discussion.

*1. When is sex permissible? (God created sexual activity for the one-flesh union described in Genesis 2. It is a gift for the expression of love in marriage.)*

*2. When is sex not beneficial? Why not? (All sex acts outside of the one-flesh union is sexual immorality—sin. Sin is a demonstration of our natural rejection of God.)*

*3. What happens when two people engage in sex? (Sexual intercourse goes way beyond the other touching, sharing, and communicating that takes place between people. The Bible describes it as uniting in one flesh. It is an intimate act, inappropriate between strangers or even close friends. Therefore God condemns casual sex and prostitution.)*

*4. Why is sexual control so difficult to practice? (Sexual attraction has a spiritual dimension. It is therefore subject to active assault by Satan. In addition, our human nature seems always open to sin.)*

*5 and 6. What does it mean that "your body is a temple of the Holy Spirit"? What does it mean that we have been "bought with a price"? (Paul makes a similar point with each of these phrases [and verse 14]—Christians have the power of Christ present in them through the Holy Spirit. Christ's power working in us enables us to resist temptation to sin. His power assures us of the forgiveness Christ bought for us on the cross through His suffering and death. See also Romans 6:6–14.)*

Throughout this discussion emphasize that God clearly has a goal for sex within marriage, not outside of it. God has given us sexual desire. He has given us His Son, Jesus, to ensure our forgiveness for all the ways in which we sin. He will also provide self-control so that by God's grace offered in His Word and Sacraments we may have mastery over our temptations.

## CLOSING (5 MINUTES)

Read aloud 2 Corinthians 5:14–21. Then pray aloud this prayer: "Father, You have made it clear that You hate sin but love sinners. Thank You for forgiving our sins. Help us to accept Your forgiveness for sexual sin and to communicate Your love and forgiveness to those we know who are guilty of sexual sin. We pause for a few moments to name them in our hearts before You. (Pause for 10 to 15 seconds.) Be with us when we face sexual temptation. Give us the strength to do what is right. Thank You for making us new creations in Christ! In His name. Amen."

# 2. too little of a good thing

## sex and the media

*List sexual messages and attitudes promoted by various media (TV, radio, movies, teen magazines, etc.).*

## sex and teen culture

*List the various attitudes toward teen sex at your school and attach a percentage to each attitude.*

## sex and god's word

*1. Read **1 Corinthians 6:12–20**. What does Paul say about sexual relations? What benefit is it to be "a temple of the Holy Spirit"?*

*2. Read **Psalm 51:1–17**, which David wrote after being confronted with his sin of adultery with Bathsheba. Whom does David say he has sinned against? What does David ask for? What are the "sacrifices" God wants from us for our sins? How are we able to do this or anything else God desires?*

*3. Read **Psalm 103:8–12**.*
*What does God promise to those who confess their sin(s)?*

sexual boundaries

sexual purity

# bonus student page

*Read* ***1 Corinthians 6:12–20****. Discuss the following questions.*

1. *When is sex permissible?*

2. *When is sex not beneficial? Why not?*

3. *What happens when two people engage in sex?*

4. *Why is sexual control so difficult to practice?*

5. *What does it mean that "your body is a temple of the Holy Spirit"?*

6. *What does it mean that we have been "bought with a price"?*

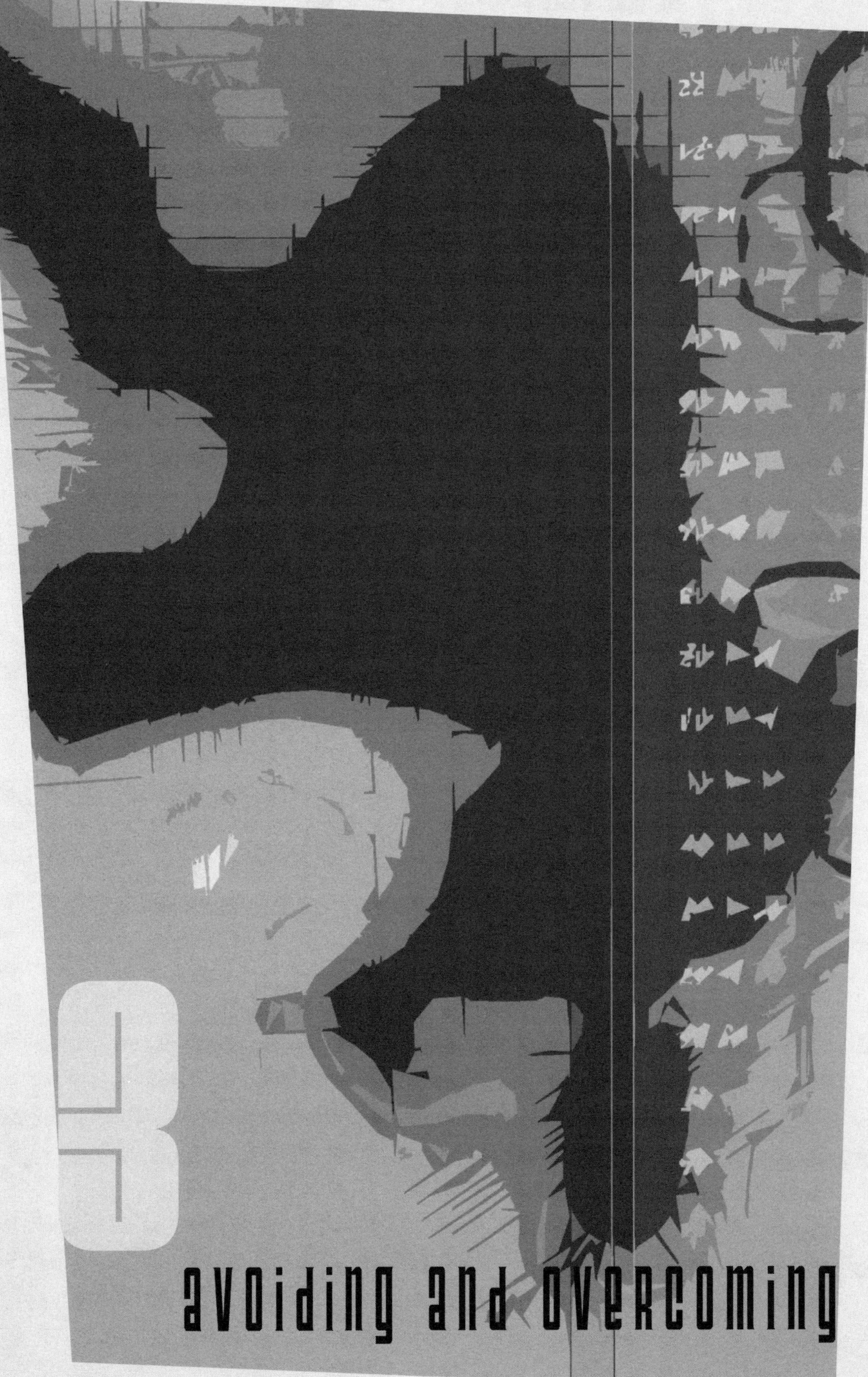

# 3 avoiding and overcoming

temptations

## LESSON FOCUS

Temptations toward evil abound for all people including teens. God in His Word provides rescue for those who are caught by temptation and resources for resisting temptation. God's Law warns us to flee temptation and resist it. But the Law alone does not provide the ability to turn our selfish human nature away from temptation.

## GOSPEL FOCUS

God offers His great love in Christ to forgive our sin and to give us new strength to resist evil and "walk in the light."

## Lesson Outline

| ACTIVITY | SUGGESTED TIME | MATERIALS NEEDED |
|---|---|---|
| *Temptations All Around* | *5 minutes* | *Newsprint or paper, markers, tape* |
| *Why Temptations?* | *15 minutes* | *Copies of Student Page, Bibles* |
| *"Promise" Passages* | *10 minutes* | *Copies of Student Page, Bibles* |
| *Running the Race* | *15 minutes* | *Copies of Student Page, Bibles* |
| *Closing* | *5 minutes* | *Bible* |

## TEMPTATIONS ALL AROUND (5 MINUTES)

Write potential sources of temptation for young people—parties, gossip, stealing, money, lying, sex, status, power, anger, cheating, friends, music, laziness, movies, TV, driving, and school—on newsprint or sheets of paper; post them around the room.

As students arrive, ask them to look at and think about the sources of temptation you have posted. Invite them to add others. Open with a prayer such as this one: "Heavenly Father, be with us during our study today. Empower us as the Spirit works through Your Word to recognize and resist temptation. Lead us to know and do Your will. Keep us from all harm and danger through the grace shown to us in Jesus. Amen."

Give each student a pen or marker. On the papers posted about the room participants are to mark the five biggest temptations they think teens face today. Remind students not to make any comments while doing so.

Identify the five temptations with the greatest number of votes. Ask, "Was it difficult to pick just five temptations? Why?" Allow time for comments. Then say, "Sin and temptation have been a part of human existence since Satan first appeared as a serpent to tempt Adam and Eve. No one is free from temptation in this world. Temptation is not sinful, but we sin when we fail to resist temptation. Today I hope you'll learn three things about temptation: (1) why it happens; (2) how we can resist it; and (3) what happens when we fail to resist temptation and fall into sin."

## WHY TEMPTATIONS? (15 MINUTES)

Temptations exist for several reasons. Satan uses temptation to drive a wedge between us and God as he seeks to tear us away from Him. God allows temptations to test and temper our faith. When we give in to temptation, we sin. Then God's Law shows us our sin and our need for a Savior. God's Gospel brings us to repentance and stronger faith as we are assured of God's complete forgiveness by grace through faith in Christ Jesus.

Form groups of three to five students and distribute copies of the Student Page. Assign each group one or more of the Bible passages found in this section. Direct the students to discuss the questions and prepare a response to share with the class. After a few minutes, give each group time to report. Include the following comments in the discussion.

> Luke 4:1–13 records the temptation of Jesus. Satan first tests (tempts) Jesus to use His divine power to satisfy His human need. Then Satan tempts Jesus to avoid the suffering and death God has planned and take an easier way to reign supreme. Satan then tempts Jesus to test God's faithfulness and protection and to gain self-importance and publicity. In each temptation Jesus calls on God's Word to resist Satan. Through God's Word the Holy Spirit works to strengthen our faith, enabling us to resist temptation.
>
> Ephesians 6:11–12 reveals that the devil seeks to weaken our faith in Christ. He uses various means, including temptations, to drive us to doubt and fear.
>
> Perseverance in James 1:2–4, 12 means remaining strong, continuing to resist temptation even when we face difficulties or trials. God can use trials and temptations to draw us closer to Him.

## "PROMISE" PASSAGES (10 MINUTES)

Say, "Think about a recent time you faced one of the top temptations listed earlier. Did you resist or give in? If you resisted, what helped you do so?" (Students may say fear of punishment, desire to respect authority, or "I knew it was wrong.") "If you gave in, what might help you resist next time?" (Students may say being with different people, remembering the negative consequences, remembering their parents' desires for them, or recalling God's Word.)

Have each small group read and report on one of the "promise" passages from the Student Page. Make the following points clear:

1 Corinthians 10:13—God provides a way out of temptation.

Colossians 1:9–14—We share in the kingdom of heaven through faith in Christ our Savior.

Ephesians 1:7–8—When we give in to temptations and fall into sin, God promises to forgive sins for the sake of His Son, Jesus.

Hebrews 4:14–16—Christ faced temptation, and as our High Priest He won our promised salvation. Because of His work, we can approach our gracious God with confidence.

Then say, "As we are tested and undergo trials, we can find strength in God's Word to resist. When we fail to resist temptation and fall into sin, we recall God's promise in 1 John 1:9: 'If we confess our sins, He is faithful and fast and will forgive us our sins and purify us from all unrighteousness.' Jesus' love and forgiveness gives us strength to resist future temptations.

"When we have a particular temptation or sin that follows us, we can also get help by seeking forgiveness and strength to resist temptation from those who share God's Law—a pastor, youth director, or other trusted adult."

## RUNNING THE RACE (15 MINUTES)

Read aloud Hebrews 12:1–3. Direct the small groups to discuss the final questions on the Student Page. After a few minutes invite responses from each group. Add these comments if others do not share them.

*1. What is the race? (The race starts with our Baptism and ends in heaven. It is our spiritual journey with Christ.)*

*2. Who is included in the "cloud of witnesses"? (The "cloud of witnesses" includes all the saints from time past who belong to Christ's kingdom. They provide us encouragement and hope as we recall that they have been through great temptations, been strengthened by their faith in Christ, and now enjoy eternal life.)*

*3. What are the hindrances we must throw off? (The hindrances include the temptations with which we struggle and the sin that results when we are unable to resist them.)*

*4. How do we throw off things that entangle and hinder us? (As we remember our Baptism, pray, partake of the Lord's Supper, confess our sins and receive forgiveness, and read God's Word, the Holy Spirit works in our lives and enables us to throw off that which would destroy us and our faith.)*

*5. How does it help to fix our eyes on the goal? (At the finish of the race is our ultimate goal, eternal life promised through faith in Christ. Point out that the power to run the race and resist temptation comes only from Jesus, our strength and hope.)*

## CLOSING (5 MINUTES)

Read Romans 8:26–28. Ask the students to pray with you and to keep in mind their struggles with temptations and the promises of mercy and hope from God. Tell them there will be a time in the prayer for them to approach God with special concerns. Conclude with a prayer such as this one: "Dear Father, You are a loving and merciful Lord. Surround us with the security of Your love and the hope of Your salvation. Help us in our daily struggles with temptations, especially these we name before You now. (Allow a time for silent or spoken prayers.) Guide us, Lord, to do Your will, to resist sin and evil, and to look for the good that You bring to us every day. Help us to remain faithful to You in all trials and times of testing. Help us in our weakness to find strength in You. Through Jesus, our Savior, who gives us hope and comfort. Amen."

# 3. Avoiding and Overcoming

## Why Temptations?

*Read **Luke 4:1–13.** Who is tempted?*

*How is He tempted?*

*How does He resist temptation?*

*Read **Ephesians 6:11–12.** What is the source of evil, sin, and temptations?*

*What schemes does the devil try on us?*

*Read **James 1:2–4, 12.** What is "perseverance"?*

*How does God use trials and temptations to increase our perseverance?*

## "Promise" Passages

***1 Corinthians 10:13***

***Colossians 1:9–14***

***Ephesians 1:7–8***

***Hebrews 4:14–16***

## Running the Race

*Read **Hebrews 12:1–3.***

1. *What is the race?*
2. *Who is included in the cloud of witnesses?*
3. *What are the hindrances we must throw off?*
4. *How do we throw off things that entangle and hinder us?*
5. *How does it help to fix our eyes on the goal?*

# 4 What do i do?

## LESSON FOCUS

Anger is real. God built this emotion into us at the time of creation. Anger in itself is not bad. What we do with our anger can be sinful. Uncontrolled anger can hurt feelings and destroy relationships.

## GOSPEL FOCUS

Through Christ, God restores our broken relationship with Him, forgives us when we hurt others in our anger, and enables us to use our anger in appropriate ways.

## Lesson Outline

| ACTIVITY | SUGGESTED TIME | MATERIALS NEEDED |
|---|---|---|
| *My Anger* | *10 minutes* | *New articles, copies of Student Page, newsprint and marker* |
| *God's Anger* | *20 minutes* | *Copies of Student Page, Bibles* |
| *How Will I Handle My Anger?* | *15 minutes* | *Copies of Student Page, Bibles* |
| *My Personal Contract* | *5 minutes* | *Copies of Student Page* |
| *Closing* | *5 minutes* | *Paper and markers* |

## MY ANGER (10 MINUTES)

Before class gather news articles that relate to anger—crimes, protests, demonstrations, and so forth. Post the articles on the walls or bulletin boards around the room or give them to students to read and pass along as they arrive. Informally discuss the articles with students. Ask, "Were the actions appropriate? "Have you ever been angry enough to participate in a protest? Have you ever hurt someone out of anger?"

Call the class together and distribute copies of the Student Page. Direct the students to the "My Anger" situations. Several suggestions are given. You may want to add students' ideas to this list. Write them on the board or newsprint. Once you have developed a list of four or five additional items, have the participants choose the situation that makes them most angry and explain the reason for their choice.

Try an "expressive" voting technique—students shaking their fists, growling, or stomping their feet to indicate their choice.

Or ask, "Have you ever 'counted to 10' when you were angry? How far would you have to count if (read the situation)." Tabulate the results. Assure students that anger is okay. Anger is an emotion. What we often do with our anger, however, can make it sinful.

## GOD'S ANGER (20 MINUTES)

For this activity, it is helpful to have small groups of three to five students. Instruct each group to read the Scripture references and then discuss the questions that follow. After 15 minutes, or when all small groups are nearly finished, call everyone back together and ask each group to share what they discovered.

Exodus 32:7–10 speaks of God's righteous anger over the sins of the people of Israel. God condemns all sin. (See also Romans 6:23.)

Romans 5:6–11 tells of God's answer to sin. He sent Jesus Christ into this world to suffer and die for all sinners so that they might receive complete forgiveness of sin, including the sinful use of anger. Repentant sinners receive the blessings Christ earned—forgiveness and eternal life.

## HOW WILL I HANDLE MY ANGER? (15 MINUTES)

Direct the students to the third part of the lesson. Tell them, "God's forgiveness in Christ empowers us to use our anger in God-pleasing ways. In Proverbs God provided King Solomon with wisdom about anger. Read the passages listed on the Student Page and then write some guidelines for anger." Have the students work in small groups or independently. Remind them that through His strengthening of us by Word and Sacrament, the Holy Spirit enables us to control our anger. Possible guidelines would be as follows:

* *Use gentle words.*

* *Do not let your anger get out of control. Out-of-control anger causes dissension.*

* *Do not remain angry with a person.*

## MY PERSONAL CONTRACT (5 MINUTES)

Ask the students to complete the personal contract based on the information they have gained from the previous activity. A sample response might be, "With God's help, when I get angry I will try to focus on the situation and not the people involved."

## CLOSING (5 MINUTES)

Read Ephesians 4:26–27. Then direct the students back into small groups. Ask each group to create a slogan based on these verses or other passages studied during this session. Sample slogans might include "Don't go to bed mad" or "Christians need to love one another—that means all the time." Ask each group to share its slogan. Close with a brief prayer, perhaps the Lord's Prayer. Point out that as God forgives us we are empowered to forgive others, even those with whom we get angry.

# 4. What do i do?

## my anger

*Choose a situation below that makes you angry, or list one or more of your personal "hot buttons."*

* *A parent who says no to something I really want to do.*
* *A friend who knowingly lets me down or disappoints me.*
* *A teacher who treats me unfairly.*
* *Seeing other people suffer unjustly.*
* *Unexpected happenings that interrupt my plans.*

## god's anger

*Read* ***Exodus 32:7–10.***

*Who is angry?*

*Why?*

*Was the anger proper, considering the situation?*

*Do you think God is angry about your sin? Why or why not?*

*Read* ***Romans 5:6–11.***

*Although angry over our sin, what did God do for all people?*

*Who receives the benefits from God's action? (See* ***1 John 1:8–9****.)*

*How do we respond to His action on our behalf?*

## how will i handle my anger?

*Read the following passages:* ***Proverbs 15:1; Proverbs 29:11;*** *and* ***Proverbs 29:22.*** *Then form some guidelines, using the ideas included in the passages.*

*Guideline 1*

*Guideline 2*

*Guideline 3*

## my personal contract

*With God's help, when I get angry I will try to . . .*





anger

5
Whose Values?

## LESSON FOCUS

Yes, movies and television reflect and instill values. Accepting the media's worldview—of success, of freedom of choice, of acceptable sexual behavior, to name a few—places an individual's faith in jeopardy. Young people will benefit from identifying the values promoted by the media and comparing them to the values God teaches in His Word. As the Holy Spirit works through the Word, they will have the courage and power to make wise choices when selecting movies to view.

## GOSPEL FOCUS

The Bible cautions us to avoid the impure and seek out good and noble things. As Christian young people grow in their faith through the Word, they can identify the true character of the things they encounter in this world. Thanks be to God that as we have received Christ through the power of the Spirit, we may live in Him. Christ's love at work in our hearts empowers us to avoid harmful influences and embrace those that are worthy.

## Lesson Outline

| ACTIVITY | SUGGESTED TIME | MATERIALS NEEDED |
|---|---|---|
| *Match-up* | *10 minutes* | *Index cards, program guide, tape* |
| *Movies and Me* | *10 minutes* | *Copies of Student Page* |
| *What Scripture Says I* | *15 minutes* | *Copies of Student Page, Bibles* |
| *Optional—What Scripture Says II* | *15 minutes* | *Copies of Bonus Student Page, Bibles* |
| *Applying It to My Life* | *15 minutes* | *Copies of Student Page* |
| *Closing* | *5 minutes* | *Paper, pencils* |

## MATCHUP (10 MINUTES)

Before the youth arrive, write the names of movie and television personalities on index cards. On another set of cards write the name of the movie or show in which they appear. (A television program guide will be helpful.) Depending on the size of your group, select one of the following activities using the cards:

* *On each person's back tape a star's name. Post the name of the star's corresponding television show on the wall. Youth can move around the room asking "Yes" or "No" questions about the name taped to them (e.g., Is this person a male?). They may continue to ask questions of any one person as long as they get a "Yes" answer to their question. A "No" means they have to go to another person. After five minutes everyone tries to guess the name taped to his or her back. If they guess wrong, they wait for another turn.*

* *Tape the names of stars on one wall. On an opposite wall, tape the names of the movie or show. One at a time, invite youth to match the name of a celebrity and the name of his or her movie or show. Place, or allow students to place, pairs of correct matches together on a third wall.*

* *Divide the youth into teams. See which team can identify the movie or show that each star is in as you read off the names.*

As you move into the lesson, begin with this prayer: "Dear heavenly Father, there seem to be so many influences in our world that oppose You and the teachings of Your Word. At times these influences tempt us to doubt You, the salvation You have freely provided us through Jesus Christ, and the place You desire to have as Lord of our lives. Forgive us, Lord, for the misuse of Your gifts. Keep any influence from leading us away from You. Help us to use technological advancements to bring glory to You and to share the Good News of Your salvation with all people. Today, as we study Your Word, may we grow in the knowledge of Your truth. This we pray in the name of Jesus. Amen."

## MOVIES AND ME (10 MINUTES)

Distribute copies of the Student Page. Divide the class in groups of three to five students to work through the questions. After about five minutes, invite each group to share responses.

You may find that many of your students have gone to an R-rated show and are very familiar with these themes. Guide and challenge, but don't put down or embarrass students who have attended R-rated movies or movies with questionable themes. Let God's Word speak for itself in the following section.

## WHAT SCRIPTURE SAYS I (15 MINUTES)

Invite students to work in small groups to complete this section. After 10 minutes or so, review the responses as a large group.

media

*1. Read Colossians 3:1–4. Then write a sentence explaining the change Jesus Christ, who died for you and rose again, desires to make in your life. (Student sentences should focus on the concept that just as Christ has been raised from the dead, He desires to raise those who love and trust in Jesus to a new life in Him.)*

*2. Consider Colossians 3:5–9. List behaviors that are evidenced, and at times even glorified, in the lives of those who do not believe in Jesus as their Savior. (Behaviors that run counter to the Christian life, as listed in Colossians 3:5–9, include the following: sexual immorality, impurity, lust, evil desires, greed, anger, rage, malice, slander, filthy language, and lying.)*

*3. Colossians 3:10–17 describes some characteristics the Spirit of God brings about in the lives of those who believe in Jesus. List these below. (Characteristics the Holy Spirit brings to the lives of the faithful forgiven who are being renewed in the image of the Creator include compassion, kindness, humility, gentleness, patience, forgiveness, love, unity, peace, thankfulness, and wisdom.)*

## OPTIONAL—WHAT SCRIPTURE SAYS II (15 MINUTES)

Distribute copies of Bonus Student Page 5. Read, or have volunteers read, Matthew 15:1–20 and Philippians 4:8–9. Have the students answer the Bonus Student Page questions individually and then share their responses in their small groups. After about seven minutes, invites groups to share with the entire class. The following comments will help guide discussion.

* *The Pharisees were concerned with outward adherence to Jewish ceremonial and dietary laws. Jesus was concerned about the "inside" spiritual condition of people. Movies could result in spiritual "uncleanness"—sin—as they influence our actions and choices.*

* *Young people will likely be able to give both positive and negative examples of movies. It may be beneficial to ask whether they see more "good" movies or "bad" ones and why.*

* *In Philippians 4:8–9 God teaches us that whatever we put into our mind and heart will influence our lives. The things that we absorb—especially the messages that we see and hear through the media—become part of our experience. They can affect our future choices, decisions, and actions.*

Remind students that God offers freely His forgiveness in Jesus as we repent of the bad choices we make. God's love for us in Christ motivates us to make wise, God-pleasing choices in all areas of our lives, including the movies we choose to watch.

## APPLYING IT TO MY LIFE (15 MINUTES)

Ask youth to keep in mind the sections from Scripture they have just studied as they think about movies and television. Here is a chance for them to become critics. Allow time for them to list shows that could influence their spiritual lives positively and those that could influence them negatively.

As you review their lists, guide the youth to understand that a show is not good just because it is entertaining. Each show has a message! Is the message compatible with the Christian's point of view or with that of the world? Ask students to give examples of negative behaviors describing the earthly nature as they find them in popular television shows or movies. (For example, *Will and Grace*, *American Pie*, and *Friends* entertain while projecting many unscriptural messages about homosexuality, children, and marital relationships.)

Talk about the opportunities the media provides for witnessing to the power of Jesus and His saving Gospel in people's lives. Ask students to give examples. Students may contribute examples of stories or interviews with famous personalities that provided a Christian witness.

Brainstorm with youth ways in which they, as God's children, can honor God through their use of television and other media. Ideas might include carefully planning their viewing and discussing attitudes and behaviors seen on television and in movies, evaluating what they see and hear according to God's Word. Stress the power of the Holy Spirit at work through the Gospel, moving them to honor God in how they use or regard the media.

## CLOSING (5 MINUTES)

Allow time for students to write prayers thanking God for the blessings He has provided through television and other modern media. Ask His forgiveness for the misuse of these blessings and for His help in using them and encouraging others to use them to His glory. Invite students to read their prayers aloud for your closing. Conclude in Jesus' name.

# 5. Whose Values?

## movies and me

1. How are you affected when you hear a movie or TV show bash your faith in God?

2. Does it bother you when you see nude or sexually explicit scenes, violence, or cursing and swearing in a movie? Which bothers you most? When might these things be a problem? Why?

3. Agree/Disagree: "Watching movies changes the way I think and act in regard to violence, sex, family relationships, and the like."

## What Scripture says i

1. Read **Colossians 3:1–4.** Then write a sentence explaining the change Jesus Christ, who died for you, and rose again, desires to make in your life.

2. Consider **Colossians 3:5–9.** List behaviors that are evidenced, and at times even glorified, in the lives of those who do not believe in Jesus as their Savior.

3. **Colossians 3:10–17** describes some characteristics the Spirit of God brings about in the lives of those who believe in Jesus. List these below.

## applying it to my life

In the space below list four movies or television programs that, in your opinion, influence your Christian life in a positive way. Now list four shows/programs that have influenced your Christian life in a negative way. Be prepared to explain your choices.

Positive shows: Negative shows:

# bonus student page

## What Scripture Says II

*Read **Matthew 15:1–20.** Summarize the Pharisees' concern and Jesus' response.*

*In what way could movies or television contribute to a similar problem of "uncleanness" in our lives?*

*Read **Philippians 4:8–9.** How do the movies that are popular today stack up against these verses? Give specific examples of positive and negative values from movies with which you are familiar.*

*Describe a time you acted out what you experienced through a movie or acted differently because of a movie you saw.*

# 6

# Whose Version of Reality?

television

## LESSON FOCUS

Like the public forums in which the apostle Paul spoke during his journeys, television talk shows and reality-based programming have become open forums where any subject can be raised and dissected, any opinion expressed, any lifestyle made acceptable, and any behavior made to appear normal. In His Word God has given us standards by which we are to live. They are not subject to popular opinion or majority vote.

## GOSPEL FOCUS

As we grow in His Word, God empowers us to recognize His good and gracious will, forgives us when we fail, and empowers us in Christ to resist the temptation to disobey.

## Lesson Outline

| ACTIVITY | SUGGESTED TIME | MATERIALS NEEDED |
|---|---|---|
| *Lights, Camera, Spill Your Guts* | *10 minutes* | *TV/VCR, videotaped segments of various TV shows (optional)* |
| *You're On!* | *10 minutes* | *None* |
| *Tune In (Alternate Activity)* | *10 minutes* | *None* |
| *God's Perspective* | *15 minutes* | *Copies of Student Page, Bibles* |
| *Truth Seeking* | *15 minutes* | *Copies of Student Page, Bibles* |
| *Bonus Activity—Were You There?* | *15 minutes* | *Bibles* |
| *That's a Wrap!* | *5 minutes* | *None* |

## A NOTE TO THE LEADER

To add emphasis to the lesson, select a television talk show or reality-based show and tape a section of it. Be selective, however. Do not tape or show material that could be truly offensive.

## LIGHTS, CAMERA, SPILL YOUR GUTS (10 MINUTES)

Greet each person as he or she arrives. If you have a videotaped segment from one or more television shows, have the tape running as an attention-getter when people arrive. Don't comment on the content. Just let the tape draw your students in. This will set the mood for today's topic. When you are ready to begin, ask, "What television talk shows or reality-based shows have you seen recently? Who were the hosts? What were the topics?"

OR

Ask for volunteers to role-play a TV talk show host and one or more guests. Encourage appropriate humor and creativity. Audience participation is acceptable too! Be careful not to "bail out" the role players too soon if there is a lull. Let their "audience" add to the creative flow.

## YOU'RE ON! (10 MINUTES)

Guide the whole group in discussing the questions. Accept each response, but encourage explanations and other opinions.

* *How "real" are the guests on talk shows? Why?*

* *What do talk-show hosts look for in their guests?*

* *If you were asked to be on a TV talk show, what would you talk about?*

* *What would you avoid talking about?*

* *If you could host a talk show, whom would you like to have as a guest? Why?*

* *If you could interview Jesus on a TV talk show, what one question would you ask Him? Why?*

## ALTERNATE ACTIVITY—TUNE IN (10 MINUTES)

Ask, "Does television reflect the truth about American society?" Then ask, "Generally speaking, does television viewing contribute to or distract from your spiritual health?" Allow the questions to go unanswered unless there are eager volunteers.

Display the following questions on newsprint or on the board. Invite the class to discuss them in groups of three to five students.

* *How are characters who have religious beliefs treated?*

* *How are men presented?*

* *How are women presented?*

* *How are minorities presented?*

* *To what do you credit the appeal of "reality" shows?*

* *What impact does advertising have on television programming?*

Invite reports from each small group. Challenge students to give examples to support their opinions. Invite students to suggest counter-examples and discuss whether the positive outweighs the negative in the TV shows they watch.

## GOD'S PERSPECTIVE (15 MINUTES)

Provide Bibles for each student. Read Ephesians 5:8–20. Create small groups of students. Distribute copies of the Student Page. Have groups write three talk-show topics on their paper. Then allow about 10 minutes for each group to discuss the Student Page questions.

Reassemble the class into a large group. Invite each small group to share responses to one of the four questions on the Student Page. Amplify their comments with the following:

*1. "Goodness, righteousness and truth" are often lacking, or even ridiculed, when talk-show guests are chosen and topics are discussed because the topics are generally intended to titillate or scandalize. Students may specifically identify where topics discussed miss God's standards of decency and civility.*

*2. Any topic could conceivably be handled from a Christian point of view, if we recognize our sinfulness and need for God's redeeming love in our lives and seek His direction in handling scandals, embarrassment, and pride. The Bible itself included scandalous stories of humanity's sin, with the ultimate goal of revealing God's grace through Jesus Christ in spite of our sin.*

*3. Questions that pry into guests' private lives or seek to scandalize guests could be turned around by the guest to glorify God's action in their lives in spite of past sins or public scandal. Help students to see that Jesus died for prostitutes, abusers, addicts, thieves, and* all *sinners, and that His grace transforms lives. God would have us dwell not on the evil in the lives of others, but rather on His forgiveness and power to overcome sin.*

*4. Ephesians 5:8 could be used to encourage a talk-show guest to share not just the sins and scandals of his or her life, but also what God has done, through Christ, to forgive and renew his or her life.*

*5. A talk-show host could exercise high moral standards by portraying sin and scandal as evil, while uplifting the positive attributes of each guest. Sin would not be glamorized, but righteousness would be upheld in a more positive way than most talk shows currently do.*

## TRUTH SEEKING (15 MINUTES)

Divide again into small groups. Assign each group or each individual in a small group one of the Bible passages from the Student Page (1 Peter 2:9–12; Ephesians 5:1–17; John 15:1–5). Direct each group to prepare answers to the four questions on the Student Page using their Bible passage(s). It may be helpful for groups to write responses on newsprint to display for further discussion.

*1. Who are we? (Remind students that we are God's children through faith in Jesus. His death on the cross and resurrection from the dead gives us forgiveness of sin as well as His good gifts on earth and in heaven.)*

*2. What is our relationship to the world? (As part of God's family we are unique, distinct from the world and its sinful values.)*

*3. What motivates our behavior? (God's love and forgiveness for us, shown by the sacrifice of His Son, Jesus, to pay for our sin, influences our behavior. The power of the Holy Spirit, working in us through Word and Sacrament, brings about positive change in our lives and helps us to grow in our faith.)*

*4. How does this affect our TV viewing habits? (As we grow in faith, we are empowered to know and do God's will. We will recognize those things that are not edifying and avoid them. We will know what will build us up spiritually and pursue it.)*

## BONUS ACTIVITY—WERE YOU THERE? (15 MINUTES)

Role-play a television talk show. The guests are Jesus and one of His followers. The show takes place on the first Easter, after Jesus had shown Himself alive to His disciples. The host should ask Jesus' follower what they now feel and think, especially about forgiveness. Jesus' words can be paraphrased from Luke 24:25–26 and John 20:21–23. Give participants time to "get into" their roles by suggesting they read Luke

24:25–26, 45–48 and John 20:21–23.

## THAT'S A WRAP! (5 MINUTES)

As a closing, ask students to share their understanding by responding to a sentence stem: "Today, I learned . . ." Ask if today's study has altered their openness to what they expose themselves to on television. Ask, "After studying this lesson, would anyone now change what level of television viewing they found acceptable?" Close with a prayer asking for God's guidance as we live in this world as aliens and strangers.

# 6. Whose Version of Reality?

## God's Perspective

*Identify three typical talk-show topics.*

*Discuss the following questions based on* ***Ephesians 5:8–20.***

*1. Are "goodness, righteousness and truth"* ***(verse 9)*** *found in the topics you identified?*

*2. What, if anything, could be done to handle the usual talk-show topics from a Christian point of view?*

*3. How might talk-show guests use their life story to glorify God?*

*4. How can* ***Ephesians 5:8*** *bridge the gap between common talk-show discussions of topics and approaches that would honor and glorify God?*

*5. How might a talk-show host put into practice what* ***Ephesians 5:11–12*** *urges us to do?*

## Truth Seeking

*Read* ***1 Peter 2:9–12; Ephesians 5:1–17;*** *and* ***John 15:1–5*** *and answer the following questions.*

*1. Who are we?*

*2. What is our relationship to the world?*

*3. What motivates our behavior?*

*4. How does this affect our TV viewing habits?*

# 7

# Spiritual Bad Breath

profanity

## LESSON FOCUS

For many young people, hearing and speaking profanity—swearing, cursing, and vulgar language—are everyday experiences. In the media and in real life, continuous exposure may desensitize them to the reality of this sin and the negative effects on their image and reputation. While the negative social impact of profanity may be of concern to some young people, the real spiritual impact of failure to acknowledge and deal with sin—including profanity—is that it separates us from God and the forgiveness and salvation He offers through Christ.

## GOSPEL FOCUS

Christians are reminded of this sin in Scripture and are nurtured and enabled through Word and Sacrament to seek forgiveness in Christ and new life, in order to combat this spiritual "bad breath."

## Lesson Outline

| ACTIVITY | SUGGESTED TIME | MATERIALS NEEDED |
|---|---|---|
| *Profanity Is . . .* | *5 minutes* | *Board or several bars of soap and a nearby window* |
| *Watch It!* | *10 minutes* | *Bar of soap, copies of Student Page* |
| *Catch It!* | *20 minutes* | *Copies of Student Page, Bibles* |
| *Scratch It!* | *10 minutes* | *Copies of Student Page* |
| *Closing* | *10 minutes* | *Bubble soap/wand, breath mints, window cleaner* |

## A NOTE TO THE LEADER

Soap will be a recurring theme/object in this lesson. Be prepared for some cleanup. As you prepare to teach, you may want to review the section on the Second Commandment in Luther's Large Catechism and/or Small Catechism.

## PROFANITY IS . . . (5 MINUTES)

Write "Profanity is . . ." on a chalkboard, marker board, or newsprint. Have the students write short definitions around the caption. Or have them write with a piece of soap on a nearby window or piece of glass.

Hold up a bar of soap. Ask how many students have ever been threatened with having their mouth washed out with soap. Then pass the soap around and have students, when it's their turn to hold the soap, describe how they feel when caught using foul language, or what they think when they hear someone else using profanity. Some may respond that it is "no big deal." Accept all responses without comment at this point. God's Law will be shared later in the lesson.

## WATCH IT! (10 MINUTES)

Write the following on the board or newsprint for the students to consider: "Profanity is language that is vulgar, offensive, or irreverent to God." Explain any words with which they are not familiar. Ask students to compare this definition to the short definitions they wrote during the opening activity.

Distribute copies of the Student Page. Explain to the students that there are three basic types of profanity. Ask them to try matching the three types with their definitions.

The first defines *curses;* the second, *blasphemies;* the third, *obscenities.* If you think it is appropriate, give an example of each. Ask the students what is offensive about each type of profanity. Have students match the Scripture passages concerning God's attitude toward each type of profanity: James 3:10, curses; Exodus 20:7, blasphemies; and James 1:21, obscenities.

Discuss with students the impact of such language on their lives. Ask, "What impact does profanity have on our relationships with others?" (It may be offensive, make others uncomfortable, or give others a bad impression of us.) "What impact does it have on our relationship with God?" (Profanity is against God's Law. It is sin, which separates us from God.)

## CATCH IT! (20 MINUTES)

Read, or have a volunteer read, Ephesians 4:29–5:4. Have students follow along in their Bibles. Then form groups of four to seven students. Direct each group to complete the questions on the Student Page. Let them know that they will be expected to report to the class what they have discovered.

When they have had sufficient time to complete the questions, get back together as a large group and invite responses to each question. Emphasize the following points:

*1. What all is included in the category "unwholesome talk"? ("Unwholesome talk" often arises from the bitterness, rage, anger, brawling, slander, and malice mentioned in verse 31, and includes the obscenities, foolish talk, and coarse jokes referred to in verse 4.)*

*2. What are some reasons given in these verses for cleaning up our words? (The need to clean up our words is revealed because it grieves the Holy Spirit [verse 30], is not conducive to a life of Christlike love [verse 2], and is improper—a poor witness for God's holy people [verse 3].)*

*3. What reassurance are we given for when we "blow it" and let unwholesome words slip out? (We can be assured as we confess our sin that by the loving sacrifice of Christ our sin is forgiven.)*

*4. What kind of talk can we try to speak instead, with the help of the Holy Spirit? (Instead of foul language, God works in us as we study His Word so we can use words that build each other up, express kindness and compassion, and thank God for His promises to us in even the most frustrating, surprising, and painful circumstances.)*

## SCRATCH IT! (10 MINUTES)

Ask the students to complete this section silently. You can help them by sharing some possible responses.

Profanity often erupts when we are angry or hurt; it may occur most frequently in certain places or with certain people. Invite students to share possible responses (not personal responses).

Ways to alter unwholesome speech might include daily reviewing Scripture passages such as James 1:21 and 3:10, changing the subject, avoiding certain places or groups, or agreeing with a friend to help monitor each other's speech. A simple tool could be a reminder such as "That's two" (as in "Second Commandment") or counting to "two" before expressing anger or hurt. Regular personal devotions and worship are also tools for growing in the grace of God and leading God-pleasing lives.

Encourage students to identify a friend as a partner in their efforts to curb their tongues.

## CLOSING (10 MINUTES)

Choose one or more of the following activities:

* *As a symbol of God's forgiveness and their commitment to cleaning up their speech with His help, invite students who have completed the "Scratch It!" section to pass around a bottle of soap bubbles and blow some bubbles through the wand.*

* *Pass around breath mints to students as a reminder to work at cleaning up their "spiritual bad breath."*

* *Invite the students to help clean the board or window where they wrote their initial definitions of profanity.*

Close with a prayer thanking God for His forgiveness of the times we grieve Him and are poor witnesses due to our unwholesome talk. Ask for the Spirit's help in cleaning up our language and building up each other. Read responsively 2 Corinthians 6:17–7:1 or 1 John 1:5–9 as a benediction.

profanity

# 7. Spiritual Bad Breath

## Watch it!

*Match each type of profanity to its definition.*

| | |
|---|---|
| *Invocations of evil on a person or thing, often used to express anger or hatred.* | *Obscenities* |
| *Improper and irreverent use of God's name or of other sacred words, often used as an expression of surprise.* | *Blasphemies* |
| *Crude and indecent names for body functions, private parts, or sexual situations, often used as insults.* | *Curses* |

*Match each of these verses to the type of profanity that it addresses:* ***Exodus 20:7; James 1:21; James 3:10.***

## Catch it!

*Read* ***Ephesians 4:29–5:4.***

*1. What all is included in the category "unwholesome talk"* ***(4:31; 5:4)?***

*2. What are some reasons given in these verses for cleaning up our words* ***(4:30; 5:2–3)?***

*3. What reassurance are we given for when we "blow it" and let unwholesome words slip out* ***(4:32–5:2)?***

*4. What kind of talk can we try to speak instead, with the help of the Holy Spirit* ***(4:29, 32; 5:4)?***

## Scratch it!

*Times I most frequently use profanity:*

*Options for altering my speech habits:*

*Someone who can help me monitor my speech:*

# 8

# What have i got to Lose?

Gambling

## LESSON FOCUS

Gambling may seem harmless to most teens—a personal issue with only personal consequences. Unpacking the motivation for teenage gambling—likely rooted in coveting wealth, rebelling, or risk-taking—will help teens to realize that gambling is sinful.

## GOSPEL FOCUS

The realization that gambling is sinful will lead students to confess their sin and sinful motivation for gambling as they grasp God's promise of forgiveness through faith in Jesus.

## Lesson Outline

| ACTIVITY | SUGGESTED TIME | MATERIALS NEEDED |
|---|---|---|
| *Welcome to Our Lottery!* | *10 minutes* | *Two sets of numbered slips, basket* |
| *I Think . . .* | *10 minutes* | *Copies of Student Page* |
| *Cold, Hard Facts* | *5 minutes* | *Research* |
| *What Scripture Says* | *15 minutes* | *Copies of Student Page, Bibles* |
| *In My Life* | *15 minutes* | *Index cards, newsprint, and markers* |
| *Closing* | *5 minutes* | *None* |

## A NOTE TO THE LEADER

"Gambling is betting something of value as a stake on the outcome of a future event, where that outcome is determined by mere chance, and the bettors agree to pay their stakes to the sponsor and/or winner of the game" (from *A Christian Response to Legalized Gambling*, by Steven J. Kuehne, published by the Minnesota South District of the LCMS).

* *Become familiar, as you are able, with legalized gambling activities in your community or state (lottery, bingo, etc.).*

* *Seek information from agencies that may provide help for gamblers such as the National Council on Problem Gambling (www.ncpgambling.org).*

* *Seek information from a local Gambler's Anonymous group (www.gamblersanonymous.org).*

* *Examine your own views on gambling and any gambling activities in which you have engaged.*

* *Pray for God's guidance as you prepare to teach.*

## WELCOME TO OUR LOTTERY! (10 MINUTES)

Give each student a number and ask them to place something of value—money, watch, rings, car keys, house keys, and so forth—on a table in the middle of the room. Make sure that after the activity you can return everything to its owner. Put a matching number into a lottery drawing. Tell the students to imagine that they have just gambled a stake on the outcome of a lottery that you will conduct in class. Pull the winner's number out of a hat, cup, or basket, and "award" two-thirds of the value of the pot to him or her, keeping one-third for yourself as the owner/operator of the game. No one else gets anything.

At this time pray together. Ask for insight into motives for gambling and how gambling fits into our value system as Christians. Then discuss with your students the thoughts and feelings they had while they participated in the imaginary lottery. "How did you feel about the winner? the losers? Were you happy? sad? nervous? excited? What were you thinking? Were you hoping to win? Why?" After the discussion, return all items to their owners.

## I THINK . . . (10 MINUTES)

Distribute copies of the Student Page. Allow members of the class to work in small groups of three to five students to react independently to the statements on the Student Page. Have them share the statements they chose and their thoughts and feelings about the choice in their small groups. After about five minutes, invite several volunteers to share with the whole group.

## COLD, HARD FACTS (5 MINUTES)

Share the following information with your students. Include information about gambling in your state or province and your community.

* *In our country today, people of all ages gamble legally and illegally.*

gambling

* *Since Rhode Island instituted a state lottery in 1964, government-sponsored gambling has grown tremendously.*

* *The Internet now provides opportunities for a whole new segment of our population to gamble.*

* *With these increases, the number of problem and compulsive gamblers has risen dramatically.*

* *The number of underage gamblers has increased as well. Research has shown that 80 percent of 12- to 17-year-olds have gambled in the past 12 months (source: ncpgambling.org).*

Of course, underage always means illegal, and that's a problem in and of itself. Some underage gamblers are compulsive, which is even more of a problem. We're here to learn from God's Word and to discuss our thoughts and feelings about underage gambling.

## WHAT SCRIPTURE SAYS (15 MINUTES)

Read, or have a volunteer read, Exodus 20:17. The Ninth and Tenth Commandments prohibit coveting. Involve the whole group in discussing the following questions:

What is coveting? (Coveting is the desire to have something that someone else has. It is a form of greed and is, therefore, idolatry.)

Why do people gamble when there are many other forms of entertainment? (It's the lure of easy money and getting something for nothing.)

Whose money goes to the winner? (The losers'.)

Is gambling harmful? (See Proverbs 13:11.)

Read, or have a volunteer read, Luke 12:22–34. It tells us that our hearts will always be set on what we think is truly valuable.

How can gambling undermine what we think is truly valuable in our lives? (It makes us dissatisfied with what we already have. The first and easiest step to any sin is dissatisfaction with a present circumstance.)

Why, according to Luke, is gambling not necessary or desirable? (God promises to care for us. We are worth a lot in God's eyes, even though we are sinners.)

What does God offer to sinners? (His very kingdom, through faith in Christ.)

Have a student volunteer read Romans 5:8 and another read Romans 5:1. Summarize these two verses to emphasize the Gospel: "Jesus died for us. Through His death we receive forgiveness for all our sins. Jesus' love for us gives us peace—peace with God, peace in appreciating the blessings He provides, peace in knowing that He is always with us."

## IN MY LIFE (15 MINUTES)

Discuss and/or role-play one or both of the case studies. Encourage students to get into their roles. Ask the participants and class, "Were the thoughts and feelings expressed true to life? What would you have said differently?"

As you write on newsprint or a chalkboard, ask the group to help you list all the ways they have gambled. If they hesitate to share, ask them instead to write their responses on an index card. Then compile the list anonymously. Write "Luke 12:32" in big letters over the list. Emphasize that God, in Christ, has mercifully forgiven all our sins, including the sins of covetousness and underage gambling. Also remind students that through Christ we have the power to amend our lives.

Invite the class to suggest alternatives to gambling (other games, even games of chance without losing "something of value"; other activities; saving their money).

## CLOSING (5 MINUTES)

Close with prayer, asking God to remind you of His promise to always provide for your needs. Ask His forgiveness for the times you have doubted His promise and for strength to live as His redeemed children.

# 8. What have i got to Lose?

## i think . . .

*Mark the following statements with a check mark if you agree, a minus if you disagree, or a question mark if you are not sure.*

- ☐ Gambling is a form of entertainment.
- ☐ Gambling is big business.
- ☐ Gambling is a sin.
- ☐ Gambling doesn't hurt anyone.
- ☐ Gambling hurts only the gambler.
- ☐ Government has no business sponsoring gambling.
- ☐ Gambling is a legitimate source of revenue for the government.
- ☐ Gambling is an addiction.
- ☐ Gambling breeds crime.
- ☐ Gambling is harmless.

## What Scripture Says

*Read* ***Exodus 20:17.***

*What is coveting?*

*Why do people gamble when there are many other forms of entertainment?*

*Whose money goes to the winner?*

*Is gambling harmful?*

*Read* ***Luke 12:22–34.***

*How can gambling undermine what we think is truly valuable in our lives?*

*Why, according to Luke, is gambling not necessary or desirable?*

*What does God offer to sinners?*

**CASE STUDY 1**

*Ted is a sophomore in high school. Lately he and a few friends have enjoyed some "friendly" poker games. The betting hasn't been major, but Ted has lost his lunch money for the last two weeks. Somehow Ted's father knows. He has decided to talk to Ted about this. What happens when Ted's father confronts Ted?*

**CASE STUDY 2**

*Pastor Meyer recently led a Bible study and preached a series of sermons in his church on gambling. This has provoked a lot of discussion in his congregation about the issue. Bill, a recovering compulsive gambler, comes to Pastor Meyer's office one day to announce that he has begun to gamble again. He knows his luck has changed because he just won $1,000, and he wants to give $250 of it to the church. He intends to continue gambling. What do the pastor and his church member say to each other now? Should Pastor Meyer accept the $250? Why or why not?*

# 9

# god's unit of measure

## LESSON FOCUS

God does not measure sin. One size fits all. But our sinful human nature would have us believe sins are "weighted"—that some sins are worse than others. This allows some to justify themselves and their sinful actions as "not as bad as the stuff others do." It can lead others to despair as they see themselves as worse than others.

## GOSPEL FOCUS

In truth, sin is sin; all sin—any sin—separates us from God and the salvation He offers through Christ. Only through faith in Christ and the power of the Spirit can we recognize and confess our sin, rejoice in forgiveness, and gain strength for new life.

## Lesson Outline

| LESSON ACTIVITY | SUGGESTED TIME | MATERIALS NEEDED |
|---|---|---|
| *Big Sin/Little Sin* | *10 minutes* | *Newsprint, markers, blank paper* |
| *God's View of Sin* | *15 minutes* | *Copies of Student Page, Bibles* |
| *The Power of All Sins* | *15 minutes* | *Copies of Student Page, Bibles* |
| *Our Response to God's Love* | *10 minutes* | *Bibles, newsprint, markers* |
| *Closing* | *5 minutes* | *Hymnals* |

## BIG SIN/LITTLE SIN (10 MINUTES)

Write the following list of sins on the board or on newsprint for the class to see: shoplifting, murder, lying, adultery, anger, gossip, disobeying parents, seeking the advice of a horoscope, cheating, cursing. As students arrive give them a pencil and a blank sheet of paper. Ask them to rate each sin with a number between 1 and 10 according to the seriousness of that sin. Numbers 1–3 would indicate "not so serious"; 4–7, "more serious"; and 8–10, "very serious." When all participants have arrived and had a few moments to work on the exercise, say, "This exercise demonstrates how our human nature prompts us to classify sin. As we will find out today, all sin is very serious."

Then ask, "What are some other words people use for the word *sin* to minimize its seriousness?" (Answers might include accident, blunder, defect, error, trifle, mistake, or weakness.) Ask, "Does changing the name change the seriousness of the action in God's eyes?" (No.)

## GOD'S VIEW OF SIN (15 MINUTES)

Read, or have a volunteer read, Luke 13:1–5. Offer the following background information. "Some Jews from Galilee brought sacrifices to the temple. Some sacrifices required that laymen lay their hands on the sacrifice or slaughter the animal. While the Galileans were doing this, Pilate had his soldiers rush in and kill them. We don't know why. They may have broken an important Roman regulation of some kind."

Divide the class into groups of three to five students, and direct small groups to the questions about Luke 13 on the Student Page. Give the groups five to seven minutes to respond to the questions in their small groups. Then invite groups to respond to each question. As the responses are shared, include the following comments.

*1. Why do you think no one answered Jesus' question in verse 2? (Jesus' question is a difficult one. Our human nature always seems to ask at times of tragedy, "Was it because of the greatness of their sin?" His listeners may not have had a ready answer. Of course, Jesus may not have waited for a response.)*

*2. Were the Galileans slain by Pilate greater sinners than others who escaped Pilate's sword? (Jesus' answer is no. Sin doesn't come in various sizes. "One size fits all.")*

*3. Were the 18 who were killed by a falling tower in Siloam greater sinners than those who survived? (Jesus points out that all are sinners and need to repent, or they will be lost forever.)*

*4. Are people who suffer in tornadoes, floods, droughts, and hurricanes greater sinners than those who don't? (According to Jesus' words, no. Everyone is sinful, and all sin separates us from God.)*

*5. What should sinners do? (All sinners need to repent of their sin.)*

## THE POWER OF ALL SINS (15 MINUTES)

Before you discuss the remaining questions, you might include this background information. "This is a portion of the Savior's Sermon on the Mount. Here He is expanding on the meaning of the Ten Commandments. His Jewish hearers would likely suppose (as we might have earlier) that such sins as murder and adultery were the most serious of all sins. The word *Raca* in verse 22 can be translated "blockhead." As small groups report their answers, include the following comments.

*1. How does Jesus compare the sins of murder, anger, and prejudice or name-calling? (Sin is sin. One size fits all.)*

*2. What penalty does each sin deserve? Are the penalties different or the same? (The penalties in Matthew 5 are not easy to compare. We do not know what "judgment" would be. Scripture tells us, though, that "The wages of sin [all sin] is death" [Romans 6:23]. Sin is like a poisonous drink—even a little is fatal.)*

*3. Scan the rest of Matthew 5. What other sins does Jesus amplify or make more serious? (Other sins that Jesus amplifies are lust, divorce, revenge, and hating your enemies. In each case Jesus takes a sin that some people might be able to "justify" and makes it clear that all sin is equally serious.)*

*4. According to Matthew 5:22, where does sin finally lead? (Sin—all sin—puts us "in danger of the fire of hell.")*

*5. Have you ever called anyone a fool—or something worse? How do you feel about the penalty Jesus suggests? (Students will likely admit to calling people names much worse than "fool." The fire of hell may seem a little steep as punishment.)*

Remind students of the key points: sin is not relative; all sin is serious; unrepented sin separates us from God; and without forgiveness and reconciliation, to be separated from God means to be without Him. Hell is separation from God.

At this point class members may have a deep sense of guilt. Do not leave them there. Ask, "If sin a like poison, what is the antidote?" Direct them to the last question on the Student Page and to 2 Corinthians 5:21. Say, "The antidote is Jesus. Jesus fulfilled the Law perfectly in our stead and suffered and died on the cross to pay for all our sins. When we repent and trust in Christ, whose sacrifice on the cross paid the penalty for all sin, He forgives our sin and gives us life eternal with God."

## OUR RESPONSE TO GOD'S LOVE (10 MINUTES)

Direct the students to the example of David in Psalm 32 and Psalm 69:30. Say, "Remember David's sins of lust, adultery, murder, and cover-up? After confessing his sins and receiving forgiveness, David gave thanks to God—thanksgiving for the power to live the new life." Remind the students that we can live the new life in Christ only as we are motivated by the Gospel. Paul said, "I can do everything through Him [Christ] who gives me strength" (Philippians 4:13).

Direct the students (in small groups) to paraphrase Psalm 32 using language and images that are familiar to them. Give each group a sheet of newsprint and markers. If time allows, students could embellish their "psalm" with illustrations.

## CLOSING (5 MINUTES)

Sing or recite the stanzas of "Lord Jesus, Think on Me" (*Lutheran Worship* 231) as a closing prayer, or lead students in a prayer of your own.

# 9. God's Unit of Measure

## God's View of Sin

*Read **Luke 13:1–5.***

*1. Why do you think no one answered Jesus' question in **verse 2?***

*2. Were the Galileans slain by Pilate greater sinners than others who escaped Pilate's sword?*

*3. Were the 18 who were killed by a falling tower in Siloam greater sinners than those who survived?*

*4. Are people who suffer in tornadoes, floods, droughts, and hurricanes greater sinners than those who don't?*

*5. What should sinners do?*

## The Power of All Sins

*Read **Matthew 5:21–22.***

*1. How does Jesus compare the sins of murder, anger, and prejudice or name-calling?*

*2. What penalty does each sin deserve? Are the penalties different or the same?*

*3. Scan the rest of **Matthew 5.** What other sins does Jesus amplify or make more serious?*

*4. According to **Matthew 5:22,** where does sin finally lead?*

*5. Have you ever called anyone a fool—or something worse? How do you feel about the penalty Jesus suggests?*

*6. What is the only antidote for sin? (See **2 Corinthians 5:21.**)*

10
What SHOULD i dO?

adultery

## LESSON FOCUS

Sexual promiscuity runs rampant in today's society. Young people will likely know, or know of, adults who live together or have sex outside of marriage. This situation may exist within their own family. At the same time, youth learn that God forbids sex outside of marriage. They need assistance to deal with this discrepancy. Just as God expects parents to model unconditional love to their children, so also He expects young people to love and obey their parents. While sexual relationships outside of marriage are sinful, failure to honor and obey those in authority, and failure to love, are also sinful.

## GOSPEL FOCUS

God calls upon Christians, as they are strengthened in their faith through Word and Sacrament, to speak out against sinful behavior while dealing with sinners in a spirit of love so that they might receive the forgiveness offered through Jesus Christ and empowerment to live as God desires.

## Lesson Outline

| ACTIVITY | SUGGESTED TIME | MATERIALS NEEDED |
|---|---|---|
| *Sign of the Times* | *10 minutes* | *Signs prepared in advance* |
| *A Reminder* | *10 minutes* | *Copies of Student Page, newsprint* |
| *Jesus' Response* | *15 minutes* | *Copies of Student Page, Bible* |
| *Words of Comfort* | *15 minutes* | *Copies of Student Page, Bible* |
| *Closing* | *5 minutes* | *None* |

## SIGN OF THE TIMES (10 MINUTES)

Before class prepare some simple signs on blank paper. The signs should present some of the evidence of sexual immorality we see in the world around us. Possibilities: "Sex acts on TV"; "Friends say it's okay"; "Magazine advertisements entice us";

"Looking at sexually oriented books and magazines"; and so forth.

Place the signs around the classroom so that they are obvious to the students as they enter. Prepare another sign saying, "Seeing adults involved in sex outside of marriage," but don't put it up at this time.

As the participants enter, ask them to read the signs. Ask them questions such as these: "What do the signs say about our society? What effect do these temptations have on you? Are there any other temptations that are not included?" Make and post additional signs according to their suggestions.

Briefly review the feedback you receive from the students. Place the additional sign on the wall. Remind them that adults, just like young people, face daily temptation. Age does not make people—even parents—immune to sexual desires. The need for security and intimacy can tempt adults, just as it does teenagers, to violate God's commands.

Pause at this point to lead the group in a short prayer asking God to bless this study.

## A REMINDER (10 MINUTES)

Distribute copies of the Student Page. Direct them to the quote from 1 John 2:16. Ask for a volunteer to read the passage aloud. Ask, "What actions is John talking about?" Ask the students to brainstorm the specific sins to which John might be referring. Record their responses on the board or newsprint. Possible responses might include watching sexually explicit movies, lusting after people of the opposite sex, and having sex outside of marriage.

Once again, remind the students that God's Word is very clear when it comes to sexual sins. The word *adultery* in the Sixth Commandment includes a multitude of sins and behaviors.

## JESUS' RESPONSE (15 MINUTES)

Tell the students that the people of Jesus' day were just as vulnerable to sexual sins as are people today. Jesus encountered people whose behavior went against the desires of His Father.

One such encounter is recorded in John 8:1–11. Refer the students to that passage, and ask for a volunteer to read the account aloud. Following the reading, allow the students time to discuss the questions in groups of three to five. After about 10 minutes, invite reports from the small groups on each question.

*1. How did the people react to the woman? (With scorn, they dragged her into the temple.)*

*2. How do people react to those caught in immoral behavior today? (Sadly, most turn their heads the other way and ignore immoral behavior.)*

*3. What did the woman need at that moment? (She needed rescue, someone to speak for her.)*

*4. How did the religious leaders respond to her need? (They were prepared to apply the Law of Moses and stone her to death.)*

*5. How did Jesus respond to the woman's need? (He applies the Gospel, the message of forgiveness.)*

Help the participants understand that those who enter adulterous relationships often are looking for acceptance and security. The temptation is to respond to a basic need in a manner that only provides temporary satisfaction or gratification.

Focus on the final question: "How did Jesus respond to the woman's need?" Guide the students to see that Jesus did not condemn the woman. He offered her protection, understanding, and acceptance. He also sent her on her way with a reminder that while He cared for her as a person, His desire was that she stop her immoral behavior. Jesus' words of love and forgiveness for the woman would empower her to do as He commanded. Say, "This woman could have been the mother of someone like you. Would that change things in any way?" (While that may change our personal feelings somewhat, it would not change God's Word or Jesus' response to sin.)

Ask the students to think of other instances in the Bible where people have been involved in an immoral lifestyle. Examples might be King David (2 Samuel 11:1–5); Abraham (Genesis 12:10–20); and the woman at the well (John 4:1–26). How did God react toward the offender in each of these situations?

## WORDS OF COMFORT (15 MINUTES)

Direct the students back to the Student Page. Have someone read aloud 1 John 2:15–17.

What does John mean by the words "the world and its desires pass away"? (All relationships and actions in this world are temporary.)

What is meant by the statement "the man who does the will of God lives forever"? (In the end our personal relationship with Jesus Christ as our Lord and

Savior is what matters. Through faith strengthened by Word and Sacrament we are empowered to do "the will of God.")

Have a volunteer read 1 John 2:12–14. Allow the students time to work independently responding to the questions. Summarize this portion of the lesson by reminding the participants that while God hates our sinful behavior, He loves sinners. With God's strength we can demonstrate that love as we deal with those around us who are involved in an adulterous relationship.

## CLOSING (5 MINUTES)

If time allows, direct the students to 1 Corinthians 6:9–20, and discuss these verses as a review. Close with a brief prayer asking God to bless all of our relationships and for a forgiving and accepting attitude when we deal with people whose behavior might offend us.

# 10. What Should I Do?

## A Reminder

*For everything in the world—the cravings of sinful man, the lust of his eyes and the boasting of what he has and does—comes not from the Father but from the world.* 1 John 2:16

## Jesus' Response

*Read* ***John 8:1–11.***

1. *How did the people react to the woman?*

2. *How do people react to those caught in immoral behavior today?*

3. *What did the woman need at that moment?*

4. *How did the religious leaders respond to her need?*

5. *How did Jesus respond to the woman's need?*

## Words of Comfort

*Read* ***1 John 2:15–17.***

*What does John mean by the words "the world and its desires pass away"?*

*What is meant by the statement "the man who does the will of God lives forever"?*

*Read* ***1 John 2:12–14.***

*How is this Good News for the sinner?*

*How is this Good News for the people they hurt or offend?*

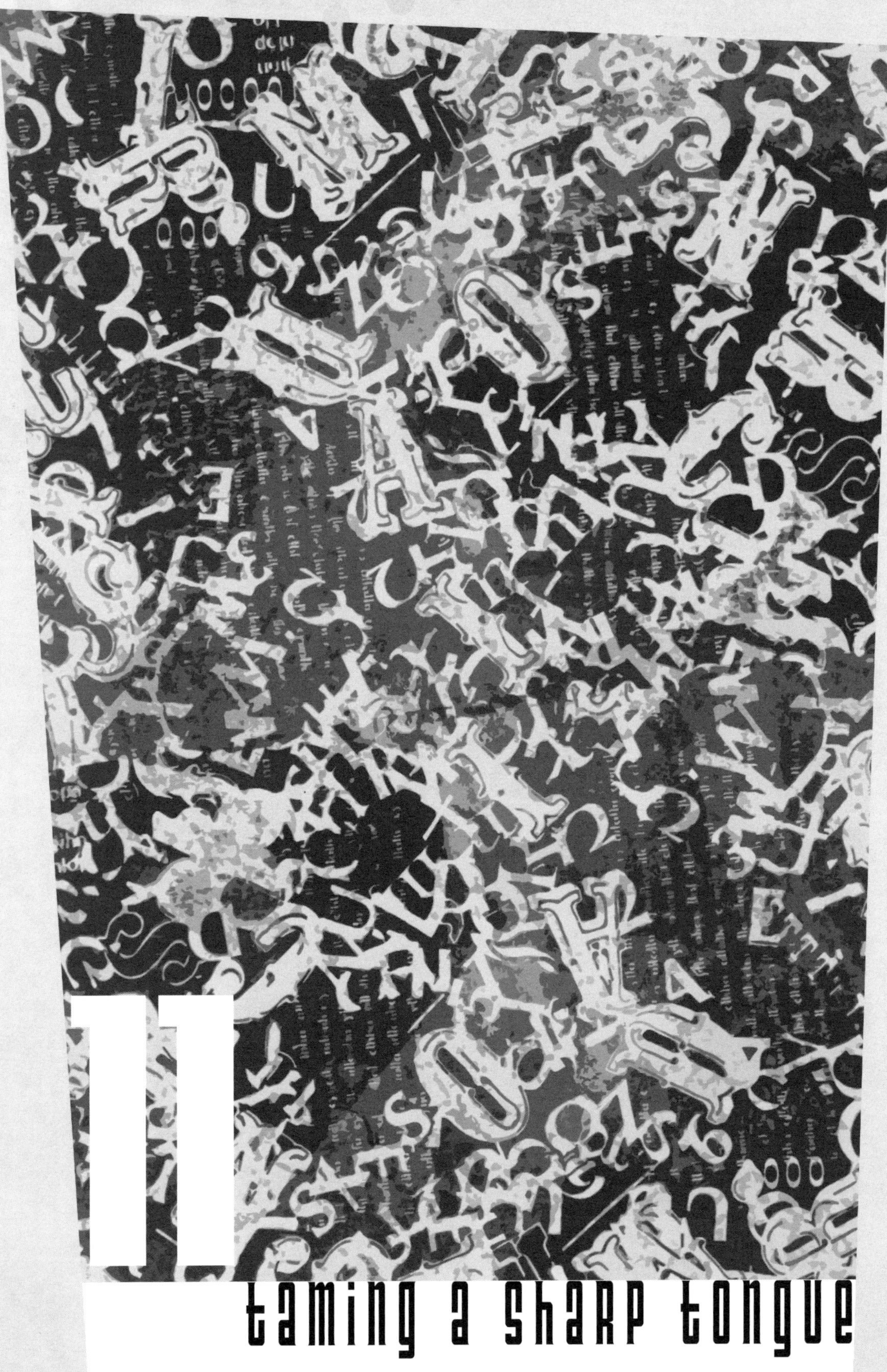

# 11

# taming a sharp tongue

## LESSON FOCUS

Young people live in a put-down culture, where status can be accumulated by the ability to "score points" at the expense of others. Like gossip, this sin of the tongue may be difficult for young people to acknowledge and combat. Those who fail to recognize their sin need to hear the Law proclaimed. This is a necessity as we encourage teens to see some common behaviors as sinful.

## GOSPEL FOCUS

As we proclaim Jesus' death and resurrection to repentant teens, the Holy Spirit motivates them to use their tongues in positive ways with their friends and family. As the Spirit works through Jesus' forgiveness, young people can grow to recognize sarcasm and put-downs as sinful, and instead use their words to speak well of others and encourage them.

## Lesson Outline

| ACTIVITY | SUGGESTED TIME | MATERIALS NEEDED |
|---|---|---|
| *Opening* | *15 minutes* | *Self-sticking notes or index cards and tape, or hammers and disposable aluminum pans* |
| *How Does It Feel . . .?* | *10 minutes* | *Copies of Student Page, Bibles* |
| *James's View* | *10 minutes* | *Copies of Student Page, Bibles* |
| *Taming Sharp Tongues* | *15 minutes* | *Copies of Student Page, Bibles* |
| *Closing* | *5 minutes* | *Songbooks* |

## OPENING (15 MINUTES)

Choose one of the following activities:

Prior to class obtain a pad of self-sticking notes or index cards and tape. Write two affirming messages for each student on the notes or cards. Possible messages: "You look nice today." "You are an important part of our class." "I really like your positive attitude."

As the students arrive for class, greet them by name. Share an affirming message with them as you attach the note with the same statement to them. Immediately move on to another person using the same procedure. You may share a second message with each person if there is time. Try to do this in a casual manner, visiting with your class as you move about the room.

When you've had a chance to greet all the students, and you are ready to begin the session, ask, "What was different about the last few minutes? How did you feel about my comments? Were they surprising to you? Why?"

OR

Form groups of four to seven students. Ask each group to sit in a circle. Place a disposable aluminum pan (a pie pan or small roaster would work) and a hammer in the center of the circle. You will need a pan and hammer for each group

Ask the participants to think of negative things they have heard people say to each other. Examples might be "You're a loser" or "You'll never amount to anything." When you instruct them to begin, they are to use the hammer to strike the pan while they state a negative comment. Choose someone in each group to go first. After one minute stop the activity. Request that the students now put down the hammer and pick up the pan. As a group they should now try to bend the pan back into its original shape.

After a brief time, ask the following questions of the whole group:

*1. Was it possible to get the pan back into perfect shape?*

*2. What marks were left on the pan?*

*3. Is it possible to use this pan for its intended purpose?*

*4. What connection did you make between the words you were saying and the action of striking the pan? (Words have an impact on people, even though we may not be able to see the effect.)*

Inform the students that today they are going to consider how the language they use can affect other people. A sharp tongue can be a dangerous weapon. Like hammer blows on a soft pan, hurtful remarks leave a mark on people.

Ask a volunteer to read aloud Ephesians 5:18b–20. Then offer a prayer such as this one: "Heavenly Father, You have made each one of us special. Sometimes, however, we let differences come between us. When that happens we can use words to hurt each other. Be with us today and work through Your Word to bring about change in the lives of those who have faith in You, especially in how we act and what we say to others. Amen."

## HOW DOES IT FEEL . . . (10 MINUTES)

Distribute copies of the Student Page. Ask the participants to reflect on the opening activity and to record their responses to the questions on the Student Page. Give them a few minutes to complete the responses, and then share them in groups of four to seven. Point out that in our society the put-downs usually far outnumber the compliments. Ask them to consider what the consequences of such actions might be. Some possible responses might be low self-esteem and general distrust of other people.

## JAMES'S VIEW (10 MINUTES)

James was a first-century church leader. As the head of the church in Jerusalem he had a lot of experience working with people. He experienced firsthand how differences of opinion and personal infighting can damage the church. His Epistle addresses many of the human issues that can affect the fellowship of believers.

Direct the students to James 3, and ask someone to read verses 9–10. Following the reading ask the class members to complete the two "reality" statements by filling in the blanks. For the first statement the word *sin* is the preferred answer, but *wrong* or a similar word is also appropriate. The second statement should read, "God *forgives* sins of the tongue if we are truly *repentant*."

Remind the students that in light of James's statement, "My brothers, this should not be," we need help in order to change our behavior when it comes to the things we say to others.

## TAMING SHARP TONGUES (15 MINUTES)

Read, or have a volunteer read, Ephesians 5:18b–20 again. Give the students a few moments to respond individually to the questions on the Student Page. Then direct them to share their responses in small groups. After a few minutes invite reports from each group. The comments below will assist you in discussion.

*1. What does Paul mean when he says, "be filled with the Spirit"? (Paul refers to the indwelling of the Holy Spirit, which Jesus promises to His disciples and which each Christian has through faith in Christ. He contrasts this with being filled with "spirits" [alcohol], which loosens the tongue and leads to sin. Paul does not refer to any special "spiritual" experience.)*

*2. What are some ways God can work to fill our lives with the power we need to speak and act in kindness toward others? (The work of the Holy Spirit is God's work. He works in us through the proclamation of the Gospel [sermons, Bible study, Bible reading] and through other means of grace [Holy Communion, Baptism, Confession and Absolution]. Other sources of strength may be the encouragement of Christians by family, friends, and teachers.)*

*3. What are some practical strategies for "holding our tongue" when we are tempted to put others down? (There could be a wide variety of suggestions. Encourage creative thinking. Some possibilities include memorizing Scripture, counting to 10 before responding to a put-down, complimenting those who are often critical of us, and speaking privately with those you have hurt or who have hurt you with words.)*

If you have additional time, have groups create a poster of their "best suggestion" to be displayed in your classroom or other visible location.

## CLOSING (5 MINUTES)

Sing or speak together a song that emphasizes support for one another, such as "Blest Be the Tie That Binds" (*Lutheran Worship* 295); "Brothers and Sisters in Christ" (*All God's People Sing* 78; *Singing Saints* 7); "They'll Know We Are Christians by Our Love" (*AGPS* 237); or "Make Us One" (*SS* 21). Join in a circle prayer; invite each person in turn to add a sentence prayer asking for God's help in their daily efforts to tame their tongues or give thanks for His action in their lives.

# 11. Taming a Sharp Tongue

## How Does It Feel . . .

*To receive a compliment?* *To be subject to a put-down?*

*1. Which do you prefer?*

*2. Which are you more likely to receive?*

*3. Which are you more likely to give?*

## James's View

*Read **James 3:9–10.** Based on James's words and your experience with a loving God, complete the following sentences.*

*Reality 1: To use words to hurt other people is ____________.*

*Reality 2: God ___________ sins of the tongue if we are truly ___________.*

## Taming Sharp Tongues

*Reread **Ephesians 5:18b–20.***

*1. What does Paul mean when he says, "be filled with the Spirit"?*

*2. What are some ways God can work to fill our lives with the power we need to speak and act in kindness toward others?*

*3. What are some practical strategies for "holding our tongue" when we are tempted to put others down?*

# 12

# a message you shouldn't buy

shame

## LESSON FOCUS

Too often in the lives of young Christians, Law and Gospel are confused. People attempt by means of the Law to accomplish what only the Gospel can achieve. Rather than empowering young people with the message of forgiveness and love through the sacrifice of Jesus, comments convey a kind of toxic shame that has devastating results.

## GOSPEL FOCUS

The Law indeed has its function—to show us our sin and our need for a Savior. Only the Gospel, what God has done for us in Christ Jesus, has the power to change lives.

## Lesson Outline

| ACTIVITY | SUGGESTED TIME | MATERIALS NEEDED |
|---|---|---|
| *Shame, Shame, Shame* | *15 minutes* | *Copies of Script Page* |
| *Shame Is Nothing New* | *15 minutes* | *Copies of Student Page, Bibles* |
| *Shaped by Shame* | *10 minutes* | *None* |
| *Our Perfect Parent's Love* | *15 minutes* | *Copies of Student Page, Bibles* |
| *Closing* | *5 minutes* | *Hymnals or printed confession liturgy* |

## SHAME, SHAME, SHAME (15 MINUTES)

Before students arrive write "shame" on a sheet of newsprint or the chalkboard. As students enter the room, greet them. Ask them to write a definition of shame or to write about or illustrate a situation that would cause a person to experience shame. You may have students write on the newsprint, the chalkboard, or a separate sheet of paper.

When all students have had a chance to do this, ask volunteers to talk about their responses. Accept all responses at this time without judging them. Ask "how" and "why" questions to help the students think through their responses.

Distribute copies of the Script Page. Seek volunteers or assign the principal reading parts in the drama. Encourage the students by your own participation to "ham it up." Then share the following information. "We've all experienced shame. It isn't always bad; shame is a response we feel when we sin. It can motivate us to more positive things. However, shame can become poisonous—toxic. Some people can be overwhelmed by shame. It becomes their identity. They see themselves, rather than the sinful actions they commit, as shameful. They confuse their sinful nature and the sin they commit. They lose sight of God's love and His Spirit at work in their lives."

## SHAME IS NOTHING NEW (15 MINUTES)

Distribute copies of the Student Page. Ask the students, "When did people first feel shame?" Allow students to work in small groups of three or four to read the passages and answer the questions. When most groups have finished, have them summarize their answers with the entire class. Possible answers:

*1. What in this situation caused shame? (Awareness of their sin caused Adam and Eve to experience shame.)*

*2. What keeps our shame on account of sin from becoming toxic? (God condemns our sinful actions, but offers forgiveness. Through Jesus Christ, shame does not become our identity before God.)*

## SHAPED BY SHAME (10 MINUTES)

Read the following statements to the whole group. Invite them to vote, with thumbs-up or thumbs-down, on whether the critical statement is likely to induce healthy shame or toxic shame.

*1. Kim forgot to bring her algebra book to school. Her teacher says, "I can't believe you did that! You must have a lot on your mind." (Probably not toxic, if focus is on this action. Kim is not being labeled forgetful.)*

*2. Jim flunked his algebra test and says, "It's no use. I'll never get this stuff." (Potentially toxic. Jim is accepting a negative view of himself.)*

*3. Jim's father says, "You're dumb just like your brother." (Toxic. Focus is on identity.)*

*4. When Kyle doesn't make the basketball team, her father says, "It must be tough on you to see your friends do better at this than you." (Not toxic. Focus is on a skill, not on Kyle's identity.)*

*5. Lee forgot to fill up the family car with gas after using it. His mother says, "This is the thanks we get for letting you use the car." (Probably toxic. Lee is labeled as an ungrateful person.)*

## OUR PERFECT PARENT'S LOVE (15 MINUTES)

Say, "The antidote, the remedy, for toxic shame is unconditional love—love like that of a perfect parent. Love respects feelings and gives a strong positive, personal identity. It is God's love." Ask the students in their small groups to look at one of the four Bible passages at the bottom of the Student Page. Make sure each group has a passage. Allow the groups a few minutes to identify the qualities of a loving parent that God, our heavenly Father, portrays. When the groups are finished, ask them to report on their discoveries.

Then ask each student to write a summary of those passages into an imaginary message from God as He might speak to them—parent to child. "What would He say to you? How would He affirm you? What hope would He offer?" (Students can write on the back of the Student Page.) This message is only for them; remind them to take it with them if they do not want others to see it.

## CLOSING (5 MINUTES)

Give students an opportunity to share God's forgiveness with each other. You may wish to follow an order for corporate Confession and Absolution included in *Lutheran Worship* (pages 308–9) or you may prepare your own.

# 12. a message you shouldn't buy

## shame is nothing new

*Read* ***Genesis 3:1–13.***

*Use the information you find there to answer these questions.*

1. *What in this situation caused shame?*

2. *What keeps our shame on account of sin from becoming toxic?*

## our perfect parent's love

*The Bible describes our relationship with God. Summarize the picture of God in these passages.*

***Isaiah 49:13***

***Isaiah 61:7–10***

***Luke 15:21–24***

***Hebrews 12:1–2***

# 12. a message you shouldn't buy—script page

## Shame, Shame, Shame (a dramatic reading)

*(The first half can be spoken like a chant.)*

**Satan:** Go stand in this corner if you've cheated in school.

**Reader 1:** I admit it; I did it. I'm a cheat and a fool. *(Reader 1 goes to one corner and faces it.)*

**All:** Shame! Shame! Shame on you!

**Satan:** Go stand in that corner if you've lied to miss school.

**Reader 2:** I admit; I did it. I've lied to skip school. *(Reader 2 goes to a different corner, facing away from the class.)*

**All:** Shame! Shame! Shame on you!

**Satan:** Go away to a corner if you've backtalked your folks.

**Reader 3:** I admit it; I did it. I'm a brat and that's that. *(Reader 3 stands facing a third corner.)*

**All:** Shame! Shame! Shame on you!

**Satan:** Stand in a corner if you've taken what doesn't belong to you.

**Reader 4:** I admit it; I did it. I'm a thief and a crook. *(Reader 4 stands facing the last corner.)*

**All:** Shame! Shame! Shame on you!

**Satan:** Go stand in the corner if you've wanted revenge.

**Reader 5:** They made me angry and irate; all I felt for them was hate. *(Reader 5 searches, can't find a corner, and then sits down in frustration.)*

**All:** Shame! Shame! Shame on you!

*(After a moment of silence, Jesus speaks conversationally, first to Satan and then to the readers.)*

**Jesus:** Satan, these people are My friends. I paid the price for their sins on a cross. Don't point your accusing finger at them, for they cling in faith to Me. *(Now to readers:)* You have been dishonest, but you are not a cheat. Father, forgive them. *(Reader 1 sits down.)* You lied to miss school; that doesn't make you a fool. I am the truth and the life. *(Reader 2 sits down.)* You have talked back to your parents, but you are still part of My forgiven family. Remember your Baptism. *(Reader 3 sits down.)* You have taken what doesn't belong to you, but I proclaim you innocent. Take My body; take My blood—freely given for the forgiveness of all your sins. *(Reader 4 sits down.)* Yes, you get angry and even hate. Come to Me, all who are burdened with their sin, and I will give you rest for your souls. *(Reader 5 sits down.)* Satan, get lost! *(Satan sits down.)*

## Available Now!

### IT'S YOUR DEAL—PERSONAL ISSUES

Tattooing/Body Piercing
Self-image
Maturity
Decision Making
Eating Disorders
Substance Abuse
Suicide
Anger
Leisure Time
College/Career
Personal Priorities
Opposite Sex

### DEAL WITH IT!—SCHOOL ISSUES

School Violence
Bullying
Grades
Creation/Evolution (faith challenges)
Competition
Fitting In/Cliques
Stress
Cheating
Gangs
Date Abuse
Outcasts
Campus "Bible" Groups

### PACKAGE DEAL—FAMILY ISSUES

Parents
Divorce
Family Conflict
Abuse
Blended/Nontraditional
Grief and Suffering
Co-dependency
Marriage
Blame
Teen Parenthood
Money
Mentors and Models

### NO DEAL—TEMPTATIONS

Pornography
Sexual Boundaries
Temptations
Anger
Media
Television
Profanity
Gambling
"Little" Sins
Adultery
Sarcasm
Shame

## Available Spring 2004

### WHAT'S THE BIG DEAL?—WORLD ISSUES

Homosexuality/Alternative Lifestyles
HIV/AIDS
Bioethics (fetal tissue, stem cells, cloning)
Abortion
Euthanasia
Prejudice
Natural Disasters
Poverty
Terrorism
Environment
War
Peace

## Available Spring 2004

### IT'S A BIG DEAL!—FAITH ISSUES

Faith Challenges
Worship—Elements of Worship
Lutherans and Catholics
Nondenominational Churches
Lutherans and Other Christians
Judaism
Mormons
Jehovah's Witnesses
What Brand of Lutheran?
Religious Rights
Interpreting Scripture
Care Ministry/Servanting